I AM PANTHER TAEKWONDO

I am the power that lifts the human spirit through self-improvement and personal development.

I am able to move gracefully away from transgressions, knowing the value of restraint while still promoting self-defence.

I am the life force that conveys the martial arts, and instils leadership skills required to build a strong community and nation.

I am the magnet that attracts the curiosity of the wide-eyed child and supports parents and teachers to develop a strong sense of honour, respect, courtesy and loyalty.

I am the vessel that stimulates dreams, stirs emotions, awakens creativity and encourages perseverance.

I am in the heart of the masters, instructors and students who live the core discipline of strong personal values, character and leadership.

I am the marker that defines an individual's ambition and a community's shining dreams.

I am more than a moment in time; I define moments for our future generations.

I am Panther Taekwondo Black Belt Academy.

Grand Master Ewan Briscoe

DEDICATIONS

*This book is dedicated to my
four children and seven grandchildren.*

*My beautiful wife Karlene Briscoe who
saved my life emotionally and physically.*

*In loving memory of my sisters
Beverley and Angela and my Mum and Dad.*

*Cover photos by my brother and best friend
Tyrone A Briscoe.*

*I also want to thank my publisher
and mentor Christopher Day and
my editor Liz who dotted my Is and crossed my Ts.*

KICK START YOUR LIFE

TAKING CONTROL OF YOUR LIFE AND ACHIEVING YOUR PASSION AND PURPOSE

GRAND MASTER
EWAN C. BRISCOE

Published by
Filament Publishing Ltd
16, Croydon Road, Beddington, Croydon,
Surrey, CR0 4PA, United Kingdom
Telephone +44 (0)20 8688 2598
Fax +44 (0)20 7183 7186
info@filamentpublishing.com
www.filamentpublishing.com

ISBN 978-1-912256-39-6

Printed by IngramSpark

CONTENTS

Dedications   3

Introduction   9

What others say about Ewan   13

What Panther TKD can offer you   19

Ewan's book is for you if...   21

PART ONE: LIVING   23

Chapter One: The Journey of Taekwondo   25

Chapter Two: My Story In My Own Words   43

PART TWO: LEARNING   91

Chapter Three: Grow Up Kicking: Taekwondo For Young People   93

Chapter Four: The Warrior In The Workplace   149

Chapter Five: Panther Taekwondo For Purposeful Living   197

CONCLUSION: Passing It On   221

INTRODUCTION

Nine times British Taekwondo champion, member of the 1987 European Championship winning Taekwondo team, three times winner of the Combat Martial Arts Hall of Fame Award, trainer of TV gladiators Cobra and Panther and founder of the Panther Taekwondo Academy... there's no doubt Ewan Briscoe's a fighter.

He's learned some hard lessons - and applied those lessons to life outside martial arts.

He's taken the focus and discipline of a fighter into the fields of business and education, as a trainer and mentor of young people and a motivational speaker.

He has also dedicated a lot of his time to the advancement of young children in his community, for which he has been awarded the Metropolitan Police Commendation Award.

His services have also been sought after for self-defence courses, security personnel training, and by sports and TV celebrities for personal tuition. The Metropolitan Police is looking into using his expertise to redirect young offenders toward a positive lifestyle teaching them to be masters of themselves – not victims of circumstances.

Ewan is a Taekwondo grand master, a successful businessman, a skilful mentor and a respected community leader. And to get to where he is today, along with the challenges and responsibilities of founding, growing and running a successful business, he's faced personal challenges and also confronted racism and prejudice.

Ewan now puts what he's learned into action in his work with clients of all ages, from young people looking for their path in life, businessmen and women who want to achieve in the workplace and many who are looking for the sense of personal direction and purpose which the martial arts can bring.

This book tells the story of his personal journey as a fighter, teacher and leader. Drawing on these lessons and experiences, Ewan then offers an exciting path into your future.

Ewan's mission today is to use the power of Panther Taekwondo to help people of all ages to develop the inner and outer strengths and skills they will need to face the challenges of the modern world and make a success of their lives.

WHAT OTHERS SAY ABOUT EWAN

MASTER PAUL CHAFE

Chief Instructor/Chief Referee/Tournament Director – 6th Dan

I started training in Taekwondo back in 1986 when I was 13 years old. I have been teaching Taekwondo since 1989 and have competed in both national and international competitions, winning medals at various levels in both full contact sport (korugi) and the technical (poomsae).

Since having retired from competition Taekwondo I now concentrate on both coaching and teaching.

As the chief instructor I regularly maintain my teaching and knowledge through training sessions and seminars with our founder and president of Panther Taekwondo Black Belt Academy, Master Ewan Briscoe.

My biggest accomplishment to date has been to guide many of my students from novice white belt students, through to accomplished black belts.

ANGIE LE MAR

Author/comedienne/writer/businesswoman

I've known Master Ewan Briscoe for most of my life. Growing up, Ewan was the guy who looked out for me and friends in our local area. If we were at an event/party and Ewan was there, we knew we would be alright.

As years went on, I had the pleasure of having Ewan on my TV and radio talk show. His advice to us was *'build your daughter's confidence by joining a Taekwondo class'*. On his advice I did so, my daughter's confidence soared over night, and she hasn't looked back.

There are few people who impact lives for the better. Grand Master Ewan Briscoe is one of them.

WHAT PANTHER TKD CAN OFFER YOU

Courtesy

Integrity

Perseverance

Self-control

Indomitable spirit

Ewan believes that the skills of a Taekwondo fighter make a difference not just to a person's body and physique, or even just to their confidence. The martial art of taekwondo makes a real difference in your heart.

The story of Panther Taekwondo Black Belt Academy teaches more than just martial arts skills, or fighting skills. It teaches vital lifeskills.

That's why this book contains the story of Ewan B's business and the story of his life. They are the same story. The lessons he's learned, he learned the hard way. Then he applied them – first to himself and then to the thousands of students he's taught down the years.

These skills and this knowledge can be transformative.

So now it's time to take them to the wider world: to help young people everywhere start to kick their way through life, to achievement, success and lasting contentment, and to help people who are facing setback and struggles to face up to challenges and find their path.

EWAN'S BOOK IS FOR YOU IF...

- You are looking for your path in life, or have come to a barrier and wonder how to climb over it

- You are facing challenges, whether in your personal or working life, and feel in need of inspiration

- You're a professional who wants to take your career to the next level

- You are a teacher or trainer, looking for ways to help and inspire your students

- You are asking yourself what your purpose in life really is. What have I really achieved?

It might be a big birthday, becoming a parent or facing a health scare; you might feel frightened about the future or experience regret for the past. Times of reflection and evaluation are creative and exciting as well as challenging, and you can rise to them with energy and renewed enthusiasm for what still lies ahead.

Wherever you are right now, and whatever challenges you face, this book can help you find your purpose and focus on the goals you want to achieve in the future.

Get ready to kick start your life!

"Once a mind is expanded it can never shrink back to its initial size"

PART ONE: LIVING

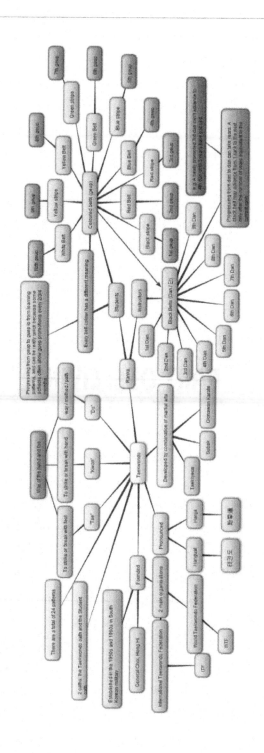

CHAPTER ONE:
THE JOURNEY OF TAEKWONDO

'Taekwondo' means 'the way of the foot and the fist'. It's a Korean martial art, characterised by head height kicks, jumping and spinning kicks.

It's a sport with ancient roots going back over 2000 years. But in Korea it's always been known as much more than a sport or a means of self-defence. It is a way of life which draws upon discipline, perseverance and other positive moral qualities.

Its roots lie in the code developed by a group of knights in ancient Korea, during a period when the country was divided into three warring tribal kingdoms. One of these kingdoms, Silla, in the south east region of modern Korea, was particularly small and weak and had many problems defending itself from its larger, more aggressive neighbours. So the knights of Silla decided that a different approach was needed.

The king of Silla formed a group of warriors called the Hwa-rang. They were trained to fight with sword, spear and bow and also in a form of unarmed combat called Soo-bak. The king, however, was aware that success in battle was not just about weapons or even about fighting techniques: mental attitude played an enormous part.

The king asked Won Kang, a buddhist monk and scholar, to take charge of training the Hwa-rang. He did so, and created a form of thought and an ethical code to unite them and focus their determination to achieve the goal of defending the kingdom of Silla.

"HwaRang became the HwaRangDo, which meant 'way of the flower of manhood'"

Won Kang's five principles were:

1. Be loyal to your king

2. Be obedient to your parents

3. Have honour and faith among friends

4. Have perseverance in battle

5. Be just and never take a life without cause

With this code of ethics and with their skills in fighting, the HwaRang became the HwaRangDo, which meant *'way of the flower of manhood'*. The HwaRangDo became known for bravery and fighting skill. They defeated the rival kingdoms and unified Korea into one country known then as Koryo.

Modern Taekwondo was developed during the 1940s and 1950s, incorporating elements of karate and Chinese martial arts with Korean martial arts traditions. The Korean word *'kwan'* means *'martial arts school'*.

The Korea Taekwondo Association was formed in 1959 and is the world's oldest governing body for the sport. Today, Taekwondo is run by the International Taekwondo Federation, which was founded in 1966 and a partnership between the two Korean organisations, Kukkiwon and World Taekwondo.

Modern Taekwondo is an international art and sport practiced by over 20 million people in 190 countries worldwide. It teaches more than just physical fighting skills and defensive techniques. It is a discipline that shows ways of enhancing our spirit and life through training our body and mind.

The beauty of Taekwondo

I am no fan of politics. That will come out in this book. As a result, I'm cautious about structures and organisations. I am a traditional martial artist. Running Panther is my business, but Taekwondo is also an art

that I love. I could just as easily teach one person in a room – for me, the joy would still be there.

I've been in classes around the world, and I've consistently found that the majority of students of Taekwondo feel the same as I do. They identify as martial artists rather than sportsmen and women – although of course practising Taekwondo has many very positive fitness benefits and can be greatly enjoyed as a sport.

The art of Taekwondo brings focus, discipline, inner balance and self-control. To begin with, I was a champion and I fought for glory. Later, I was ready to set glory aside and start teaching and inspiring others.

My biggest inspiration, other than my father, is my instructor GRAND MASTER PARK SOO NAM, 9th Dan who is one of the most popular international Taekwondo grand masters of these times.

As an experienced champion, his innovative teaching style, people-friendly approach and great experience in the art of Taekwondo brought him rapid success; over ten years, he successfully worked as the German national coach and recorded numerous titles for Germany on the international stage. For example, Germany won the European Championships five times under his leadership.

His own dojang (Taekwondo training centre) also brought out great athletes who celebrated many international successes.

He has coached over 160 Taekwondo players to international championship medal places, producing many champions at events such as the World Taekwondo Championships, the European Taekwondo Championships, the Pre-Olympic Games and the World Games.

Grand Master Park Soo Nam, 9th Dan, has sat on the ruling councils of British Taekwondo as well as both the European Taekwondo Union (ETU) and the World Taekwondo Federation (WTF).

He is a former special assistant of ex-WTF chief and International Olympic Committee vice-president Un-Yong Kim. He has also served as vice president for the World Taekwondo Federation. His latest appointment is as Honorary President of the European Taekwondo Union.

Along with him, friends like Master Con Halpin, Grand Master Mark Richardson, Grand Masters Andy Davies, Michael King, Niall Grange and especially coach Chris Sawyer have found a wonderful balance between sport and martial arts. They've inspired me down the years. I thank them and I seek to emulate them.

PANTHER TAEKWONDO: A Lifetime's Journey

At the beginning, everyone who joins Panther Taekwondo attends an introductory class. There are different lessons for children and adults because different age groups have different needs, but no other differences. We practise sport for all and we are totally inclusive.

The youngest children start at 4, but we don't accept every 4 year old. We do a dexterity and coordination test and if they are not quite ready to begin, we ask them to wait a few months.

After two weeks of introduction, if a child seems keen to begin classes, we check with parents on their behaviour at home and at school. We are looking for maturity and the ability to concentrate. If all's well, we present new students with their uniforms and promote them into a main class.

Gradings take place every three months. Rank in Taekwondo is marked by the colour of belt a student is entitled to wear. If a student passes every grading, they will progress up the ranks as follows:

White - white/yellow - yellow - yellow-green - green.

Green is the half-way stage. Once a student has become a green belt (after around 15 months of training) they are entitled to help more junior students. By this point, the skills and techniques of Taekwondo are becoming instinctive and natural to the student.

We look for students to conduct themselves with increasing self-discipline and focus, who begin to embody the five principles of Taekwondo:

With gradings continuing to be held every three months, progress continues to green/blue, then to blue. At green/blue level the student has the option to join the squad and represent the Panther Taekwondo Academy at tournaments. They are also eligible for leadership roles, and those selected wear different coloured suits: they become what we call 'red suits'.

Selection is made by the students themselves, and is by vote. The criteria for success are that you must show a helpful and constructive approach: people who've been choosing to help out in classes and play a role in supporting others. (Sometimes tutors drop a hint to students that they might start stepping up into these roles with an eye to becoming promoted to red suit – but they only hint once. Whether people act on it is entirely up to them).

From now on, the groups start managing themselves as we encourage the development of leadership skills and teamwork. Redsuits are put in charge of the lower grades. Black belts, however, always teach beginners.

Now in the higher ranks of Taekwondo, a student can earn a blue/red belt, a red belt, then red/black.

Although gradings take place every three months, technical progress is not the same in each three month period. The distance to be travelled in technical skill and ability is a little bit shorter each time as physical mastery increases, but the psychological and emotional difference becomes greater.

We look for students to conduct themselves with increasing self-discipline and focus, who begin to embody the five principles of Taekwondo:

- Courtesy

- Integrity

- Perseverance

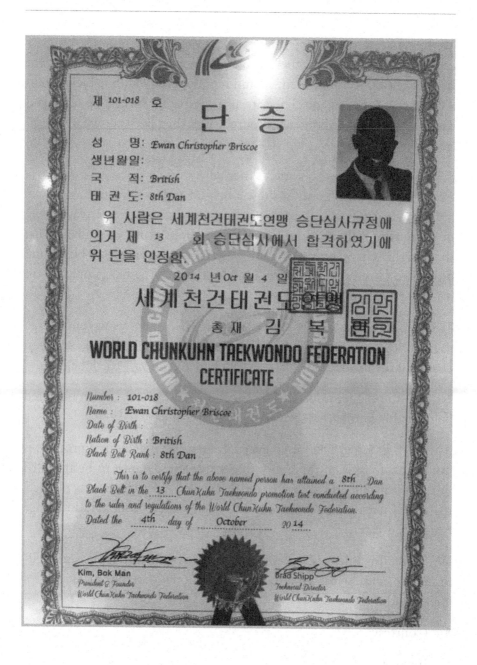

Black belts can progress up to Tenth Dan, a process which takes many years. I am now Eighth Dan.

- Self-control

- Indomitable spirit

Once a student has achieved a red/black belt, the next level is black belt and that takes longer: it's at least six months until the next grading.

Black belt gradings last at least 4 hours. At this level, you need to know every single pattern and movement of the art: around 300 moves in all. Every one must be performed correctly. If you make a mistake, you'll need to try again in three months' time to achieve your black belt.

When you achieve your black belt, you are now First Dan. After a year, you can go for Second Dan.

Now students are also offered the chance to train as instructors. Some do, some don't, and there's no pressure. Not everyone likes to teach and some are naturally more gifted in this field than others. To become an instructor is an entirely separate training. Some people are very motivated to take this path, others far more committed to becoming fighters and to the practise of the art of Taekwondo.

After three years further training, a student can reach Fourth Dan, at which point they become a Master. At Eighth Dan, they become a Grand Master.

Black belts can progress up to Tenth Dan, a process which takes many years. I am now Eighth Dan.

As you can see, Taekwondo is a lifetime's journey.

My beautiful wife – my greatest reward was when Karlene said "I do"

EWAN'S CAREER TIMELINE

1969   Started training in boxing classes

1970   Started training in judo classes

1970   Started training in Wing Chung Kung Fu classes

1973   Started training in Taekwondo life changing experience

1976   Passed black belt grading 1st Dan

1981   British National Champion

1984   Opened my first Taekwondo school

1987   Branded the name Panther Taekwondo Black Belt Academy

1988   Asked to be a contributor for Combat Magazine

1989   TV commentary for Taekwondo at the world games in Germany

1989   Combat World Taekwondo Federation Man of the Year Award presented by Bey Logan, editor of Inside Kung Fu Magazine

1992   Combat Hall of Fame winner

1992   Metropolitan Police Commendation award winner for community service

1992   Appointed marketing director on the executive of the British Taekwondo Control Board.

1992   Trainer of TV's Gladiators' Cobra and Panther

1993   Advisor to Lewisham and Greenwich Security Services

1993   Combat Hall of Fame winner

1994   Combat Hall of Fame winner

1994   Black belt 4th Dan Master Grade awarded

1994   Voted Chairman of British Taekwondo Control Board London Region

1995   Started Panther Security

1996   Awarded World Taekwondo Federation commendation for services to Taekwondo

2002   Panther Taekwondo are invited to Korea to take part in the Kyongi University TKD Tournament in Korea

2006   Awarded 6 Degree Black Belt of the Choi Kwang Do Martial Arts International

2006   Appointed as a Chief Instructor of the Choi Kwang Do Martial Arts International

2006   Appointed as a qualified examiner of the Choi Kwang Do Martial Arts International

2006   Awarded black belt 7th Dan Chung Do Kwan

2007   Appointed as UK Chairman of Haidong Gumdo (Korean Swordsmanship)

2007   TV commentary for World Taekwondo Championships in Beijing

2009   Awarded black belt 6th Degree Tyga International

2014   Awarded black belt 8th Dan Chung Do Kwan Grand Master Grade

2014   Awarded black belt 8th Dan World Chunkuhn Taekwondo Federation

2017   Appointed UK Director for the DRCS (Directive Reactive Control Self Defence System)

Proud father of four children and seven grandchildren

CHAPTER TWO:
MY STORY IN MY OWN WORDS

Taekwondo is my life. It's not just a sport, it's a way of being. It provides a set of ethical guidelines which I value, respect and always seek to follow. Over and over again I've seen the difference following these guidelines makes not just in my own life but in the lives of my students.

That's why I've written this book!

I didn't know when I started learning martial arts as a young boy that I would grow up to found my own Taekwondo school, Panther Taekwondo, and have the privilege of teaching and mentoring so many young people. I didn't know that I would become a Taekwondo champion and go on to train champions. But I did know, from quite an early age, the importance of following my own path, and I try to encourage other young people to have the same approach to life. From having respect for yourself comes respect for others.

But it hasn't been a straightforward journey. Just because you're on the right path doesn't mean that you will never experience setbacks or difficulties or that everything will come up roses straight away.

How we face challenging and difficult situations is the measure of us. It's when things are difficult that we can be drawn away from our values and end up behaving in ways that we don't feel in our heart of hearts are right. That's when following an ethical code is so very important.

My values and beliefs were primarily learned from my mum and dad, both of whom are sadly no longer with us. But my relationships with both of them are still very much alive: I think about them, I miss them

very much and I value both what they taught me and what they showed me by their example. When I mentor and teach others, I think of my parents. They were my first and in so many ways my wisest teachers.

I grew up in Lewisham, south London, in the 1970s. There were some rough and difficult times. Back then if you didn't do boxing or judo, it was hard to survive on the streets, where you had to be tough and you had to be able to handle yourself. If you couldn't look after yourself, it was easy to get led down the wrong path.

My parents were looking for something to give me focus and direction in my life. That's how my journey in Taekwondo began.

But of course, it wasn't straightforward.

ME AND MY DAD

Right from the start, my passion for Taekwondo caused some issues in my relationship with my father. He was proud of me, but – like a lot of dads – he also had some pretty clear ideas of what he expected me to do. He was a martial artist too, and had been all-Jamaican boxing champion. We were a sporting family and I knew that I was expected to take up a sport and do well in it.

Back then there was more to sport that just getting fit or having a social thing going on with your friends. When my dad was wanting me to get into these sports, he knew that what we were really talking about was lifeskills, a way of keeping me safe. You had to be tough. It mattered.

And for quite a long time, I didn't seem to be measuring up.

It wasn't that I didn't have the right attitude. I liked the idea of fitness and sport. I thought my sport would probably be boxing, like my dad, which he would be really happy about... and everything was great, until I actually tried to learn to box.

"You're going to do some sort of martial arts. That's going to happen, whether you like it or not"

I went along for my first boxing lesson. I went in the ring... great. The heavy bag, brilliant. Skipping, I felt like Muhammad Ali. Bang, bang, bang, bang on the speed bag. That was great. Then I went into the ring and I walked up to a guy. Some of you may be old enough to remember the cartoon character Desperate Dan. This guy had the chin like Desperate Dan. I was only 11; he was 16.

I only remember the times that the fist was coming away from my face. The speed at which he hit me was unbelievable: every time I went to throw a punch, I was hit. Basically, every time, bang. And I knew immediately that boxing was not for me. I just knew. Instantly.

The last hit he gave me, I actually felt like he'd broken my nose. My whole body was numb. My head was numb. Everything was numb. I just looked at him, turned away and walked outside. I remember the feeling as I was walking away. I went to the changing room, put my clothes on, and I left. That was enough boxing for me.

I didn't know how to break it to my dad. When I told him, he said to me, *"You're going to do some sort of martial arts. That's going to happen, whether you like it or not"*.

So next he found me a judo class. Once again it sounded great: I was up for it and I wanted my dad to be happy. He bought me all the gear for the judo class, just like he had for the boxing. I went there. I did this judo for about four weeks just doing normal practise. It was nice. People were throwing each other. I started training with them and they showed us all the moves.

And then I got thrown. At that moment, every last little bit of oxygen in my body left me. I said to myself, *"This cannot be right. This can't be good for you."* I knew very instinctively that this wasn't right for me and that it wasn't something that I wanted to do.

For the second time, I told my dad about it.

"I don't feel like a quitter. I don't want to be a quitter. At the same time, I wanted to be true to myself"

FINDING MY PATH

So now, at the age of just 11, I'd given up on something else. This is a theme that I'm going to be talking about later on. Me giving up was becoming a bit of a problem for my dad, and it was starting to become a problem with the way I saw myself.

I don't feel like a quitter. I don't want to be a quitter. At the same time, I wanted to be true to myself and I could feel that I hadn't found the right path for me. These things that I was trying didn't feel right for me, deep down inside, and even though I was young, I was listening to that voice and trying to follow it. But in the process, I was making my life pretty hard.

Finding the right path for you and being able to follow it is very important. Other people advise you and they might know things you don't know, so you should listen to the advice you are given with respect. When you're young, you don't know it all.

But then there's a voice inside you that knows what's right for you, and when you test the information that other people are giving you, calmly and quietly, against that inner knowledge, that's when you find your personal power and that's when you start making the best decisions for you and for your life.

It's not easy to start with. It's a long journey.

One day I saw a guy practising kung fu in the park. I didn't know that martial art existed at the time. I saw the moves and asked him what it was about. He said, *"It's Wing Chun kung fu"*.

I asked my dad if I could join. He said yes. I joined it and I liked it. It started to impress me. I liked the moves. And back at that time, this was very unusual; no one else was doing it. I remember practising in the gym and people saying to me, *"What's that? Ballet?"* They didn't understand what it was. This was the pre-Bruce Lee times; people hadn't seen these kind of martial arts moves.

"Go under, go around, go over the top,
but never give up"

So I got really into it and it became a passion of mine. When you're on the right path, you're carried further along... and so another friend of mine was doing another martial art style called Taekwondo. He told me about competitions he used to go in for. So I moved again.

After I'd moved along from kung fu to Taekwondo – really, the rest is history. I started training and eventually met the master who is still my instructor to this day, Park Soo Nam.

KEEP MOVING FORWARD

Back at the beginning, though, my dad still had some concerns. That doesn't surprise me and I don't blame him one bit.

He said to my first Taekwondo instructor that this boy has been through two styles of martial arts and boxing. "And he's given up all three", said my dad, *"so I'm going to pay you for a year. If he misses a lesson, he's in trouble. If he turns up late, he's in trouble. We can make a decision on that right here".*

So for the first few years, it was hard work for me. But after a while, I began to enjoy it.

Now I teach children in my classes to never, ever give up. Go under, go around, go over the top, but never give up. I could have easily given up, and I wouldn't be where I am today.

That's really the passion for me in the long run. The passion is to teach children to never give up, to keep focused, to never stop, to keep moving forward. So long as you're moving forward, it's important.

Some people think because they're not moving forward fast, then it's time to stop. But the time to stop is when you're not moving forward at all – then it's time for a new direction. But if you're moving forward, even slowly, keep moving forward. One of the five principles of Taekwondo is perseverance.

There's an old saying, if you're going through Hell, keep going... because why would you want to stop in Hell? That's the same thing with martial arts. Don't stop: carry on. My passion is to make sure that children in particular keep focused and keep moving.

ME AND MY MUM

Basically - my mum was an amazing woman. There's just no other way to describe her. I was lucky to be her son and I miss her every day.

My mum started a campaign called OSCAR: the Organisation for Sickle Cell Anaemia Research. Nowadays it's taken very seriously and has lots of campaigning and fund-raising going on, but historically, as a disease which primarily affects non-white people, that hadn't been the case and this awful illness had tended to be overlooked.

My mum wasn't having it. She knew her campaign needed a celebrity, so she got in touch with the comedian and actor Lenny Henry, and signed him up.

Her reputation as a charity campaigner spread far and wide. Desmond Tutu, the world-famous South African anti-apartheid campaigner, came to my house to meet her. I'll never forget the day because the police closed off the road. The writer and black rights activist Maya Angelou came to see her too.

I remember the presence of these remarkable people and the impact they made in my life and the lives of everyone around me very clearly. It was a lasting lesson, showing me the power of introducing people who'd achieved a great deal and who could be role models to my students.

BECOMING A CHAMPION

In 1981, I became British Taekwondo champion. It was one of the high points of my life.

"We bruised each other, discussed our bruises, then came back and fought again"

The championships were held in Peterborough. My coach was Pete Estoya. In the run-up, I'd trained like never before in my life.

I did training runs over London's bridges – six of them – to increase my stamina. I travelled across London from Lewisham to train in Wembley after putting in a full day's work as a graphic designer. In the changing room after training, I was so tired that I was unable to speak. The only thing that reminded me I was a human being was putting lotion on my skin after taking a shower. It reminded me that I still had a body.

On the train going home, I'd be falling asleep. One night I got home, sat down in the passageway of my house and fell asleep right there. On one occasion I'm sure the bus driver let me ride even though I had no change to pay my fare because he thought, in my wordless state of exhaustion, that I had been taking drugs.

My fellow students and I would train until we wanted to cry, bruise each other up, discuss our bruises then come back and do it again.

At the tournament in Peterborough I had lots of support from Chris Sawyer, coach and himself national champion for many years, and also from Sean Daley, Con Halpin and Lynsey Lawrence, all from a club called Brotherhood Taekwondo. My first few rounds of fighting were fairly straightforward. And so I reached the final.

Around me, there was some concern about the final: my opponent had a great reputation and was looking sharp: everyone was worried about him. My team told me to take a look at what he was doing. But I was young and confident back then – perhaps a bit over-confident. I decided it was more important to rest than worry about the other guy. So I lay back and had a little sleep instead of preparing. And then I woke up and suddenly the fight was on.

But in my dream, my brain had still been making sure I was prepared. Over and over again, I'd dreamed a double kick: fake to the body, kick to the head. If you can bring it off, it's a great move and your opponent doesn't see it coming.

*"In my dream I visualised winning,
then I went out and won"*

In my dream I visualised it, running on a loop in my mind right before the fight. I saw it as if I was a camera watching the fight from the outside, not a participant. I saw the fake, the distraction for my opponent, then the real kick landing hard. Then I saw my hand being lifted up and heard that I was the winner.

And that's what happened. I knew the kick would work. I waited for just the right moment, then I delivered it, and I won the championship.

It was a good feeling, but I wasn't euphoric. Above all, I remember feeling glad of a few weeks' rest before training began again. I was ready, after all the work and preparation that I'd done, for this new stage in my life: **being a champion.**

Being a champion changes you. It gives you many gifts: belief in yourself, reputation and respect. It also brings challenges: now you're on top, other people will want to knock you down!

It brings responsibility, too, and the chance to be a role model as younger people look up to you. And I believe it also gives you duties: to give to others, to be a positive influence in your community and the wider world, and to hand on the valuable lessons and traditions which have been given to you to others.

In my life as a champion ever since, I've set out to do all of these things.

GROWING MY BUSINESS

In 1984, with a loan from my father of £1000, I started the Panther Taekwondo Black Belt Academy. I also had a friend who put in £400 and I put in another £600 of my own money, so altogether we had just £2000.

I bought some equipment. I didn't really understand the business, so I just bought loads of suits and some equipment and paid the first three months on the rent in a youth centre in south east London.

"For a business partnership to work, you both need to move at the same speed"

After about six months or so, the chap that I started in partnership with decided he wanted to leave the partnership and he wanted his money back. We hadn't made even that amount of money but I still had to give him the money back. I lost a lot having to give him this money. However, it proved to me straightaway that there really is no such thing as a partnership if two people aren't moving at the same speed.

So, once this chap left, I was on my own and I was OK with that. I started with four students and it gradually built up to 10, then 20, then 40. Soon I had 60 students.

It was tough back then. I had to work at another two jobs. I kept my main job in graphic design for a while and I also took a job working in McDonald's fast food restaurant as well. It was all about survival, keeping Panther going and raising the money somehow.

Then in 1986, the proprietor of the youth centre where we were based wanted me to change my times for the classes, so that he could put another martial arts school in the same building.

I wasn't happy about this at all. That was totally against my principles and totally against my work ethic. I just couldn't understand how another martial arts school would take priority over mine, when I was doing so well. So we had a falling out and he said to me I'd have to leave. I decided to leave, and I went to another venue about four miles away from the venue I had been using. Consequently, I lost quite a few students.

This was my first lesson in the way that people perceived the class. Sometimes, important life lessons hurt. I believed that I would have a lot of loyal students who would come with me. What I found out was that I was just too far away for people to get to, especially the young students who needed their parents to bring them. It was a very valuable lesson.

So I moved to a place called St. Mary's Youth Centre. I made that connection straight through the vicar who owned the church hall.

*"Sometimes, important
life lessons hurt"*

PANTHER TAEKWONDO: Stable For Champions

That's when the glory years of Panther Taekwondo started. 1986, 1987, 1988, 1989 were great times for us. We as a class were winning so many tournaments that the word 'winning' and the name of Panther Taekwondo became synonymous. We went to tournaments all over England and Europe. We had quite a few British champions in the class.

We became a real stable for training champions in Taekwondo in the South East of England. I was very proud of our achievements.

Best of all, I was able to pay my father back the money he had loaned me. That was a great moment for me. It was wonderful to be able to show my dad that I'd worked hard and got to a position where I could do this.

The class had become very successful. My numbers grew and grew. I built the class up to 400 students. We were doing really well and I started to franchise out the class to other instructors. The numbers grew and grew.

Then in 1993, I went to Jamaica for a very long-awaited holiday. This is where I made a mistake which turned out to be very painful and a valuable lesson to me.

There was a young man in my class who I'd trained up to black belt standard. I'd literally taken him off the streets; he'd made some real changes in his life as a result of being involved in the class, and overcome – as I thought – some pretty serious problems including a problem with drink. I was proud of the difference in him and I thought – I still think – that he was proud of it too. He'd turned himself around.

Unfortunately, when I went away, he opened a club about a mile down the road, also called Panther Taekwondo, and told the students that my classes wouldn't be continuing because I wouldn't be coming back from Jamaica. So the class numbers fell very steeply. It's not surprising this happened: my students were led to believe that I had taken their money and left them.

"I was proud to be elected on to the British Taekwondo Control Board"

LEARNING FROM MY MISTAKES

When I came back and found out what had been going on, I was very hurt and angry. But I tried to have a philosophy that those students that left and went to him were meant to go to him, accept what had happened and move on from it.

I was proud to be elected on to the British Taekwondo Control Board (the governing body of TaeKwonDo in England) that year. I focussed on this achievement. Things were still going well for me despite this setback, so I tried not to get bogged down in blame and instead to learn from my misjudgement.

So instead of getting stuck in how angry and sorry for myself I was, I tried to respond to this setback with more hard work and I gradually built the class up to greater numbers. The numbers rose to where they were before. I was then asked to take on a class nearby in Kidbrooke where the instructor had recently left, and that class also grew very strong.

PROFESSIONAL RECOGNITION

I'd started to write for Taekwondo magazines, and built this up until I had columns in three different martial arts magazines: Taekwondo and Korean Martial Arts, Combat Magazine and Martial Arts Illustrated. As a result of this, in 1992 I was appointed marketing director for the executive of the British Taekwondo Control Board.

In 1995, I was made chairman of the British Taekwondo London region and in that capacity, I had to manage tournaments, create events, and carry out the gradings by which students progress to higher levels of achievement within the sport.

I had just passed my own black belt Fourth Dan grading, which made me a Master within the sport. I felt proud and delighted. Classes were running really well, numbers were up again and everything was rosy. I was proud of the professional recognition I now had and the reputation

"Unless you are 100% certain of people's maturity of character, don't put them under pressure"

I had built up in the martial arts world.

THE WORST TIME OF MY LIFE

In 1995 I faced my most serious setback yet, something which threatened to de-rail all my achievements within martial arts and which knocked me back personally in a terrible way.

A difficult situation has arisen with a young fighter in the class. In my capacity as London Regional Chairman, I visited the young fighter to discuss the problems and to try to resolve them. My car was off the road and I asked my brother to drive me there, which he did.

Unless you are 100% certain of people's judgement, maturity of character and behaviour under pressure, don't put then in high pressure situations. The decision I made to go there that day, and who I took with me, hadn't been such a good judgement. The situation got out of hand, with tempers flaring and voices raised. I decided that the best thing to do was to leave because people were upset, angry and were not thinking clearly. But just after I had left, my brother ended up in an altercation with the young man, and he injured him.

The young man, who was angry and looking to cause problems for me, then told the police that this injury was inflicted not by my brother, but by me. I was arrested for grievous bodily harm (GBH).

It was a horrible feeling. The police came and searched my house. They looked for weapons; they looked for a knife. This was the first I knew that a knife had been involved. I hadn't known how the young man had been injured and the shock was tremendous. This was a very serious situation. I was devastated.

I had been feeling that I'd fought my way back, overcome some setbacks and that the future had been set fair for success. I thought that I was just about to get on top of the world again. Now my world came crashing down.

"In a crisis, you learn who really sees you as you are, and won't believe bad things about you"

THREE YEARS OF HELL

The executive of the British Taekwondo Control Board sent a letter to all my students saying that I'd been involved in an incident where I'd stabbed someone and for this reason, that I had been suspended from the Board. I'll never forget reading it. I still have a copy of the letter.

Most of my students left my class, understandably enough. I was down to about seven or eight students at the maximum. This meant that suddenly the income I was making didn't cover the costs of the business.

Then hard on the heels of this professional disaster came personal difficulties. Obviously my relationship with my brother had been badly affected by the incident; I felt that he had let me down badly and jeopardised so much that I had achieved. He wouldn't own up to what he had done, and this failure to take responsibility for his actions distressed me as much as the incident itself. Our relationship came under severe strain.

This is turn put strain on my relationship with my mother; it's very difficult for a mother when her children have such a serious problem in their relationship. I understood that, and I felt for her. My sister and I also clashed over what was going on.

So my family was in crisis. I felt close to losing everything. Then our father had a stroke. I'm certain that the situation in our family and the position I was in was at least in part the cause. Shortly after this, he was diagnosed with Alzheimer's disease.

This was a horrible time for me – without question the darkest period of my life. I had to wait three years for the court case to be heard against me. They were three years of hell. The only thing that got me out of my bed was Taekwondo; I had to carry on, as the pupils I still had left depended on me to teach them.

In this crisis, I learned some important things. The people who were there for me at this most difficult time are still with me now. Those

students have now become instructors for me, and because of their loyalty, they are members of my executive team and they help me run Panther Taekwondo Black Belt Academy.

One outcome of serious personal difficulties is learning who you can trust and count on, and who really sees you for who you are and won't believe every bad word that's said against you because they've made a judgement about the sort of person you are based on observations of your character. It felt very good to know that there were people around me who would still stand by me and still believe in me, and I took strength from it.

I know that some people believe in the saying 'no smoke without fire' and whilst I can understand that, I am certain that anyone who knew me would have no doubt that I wouldn't carry a knife or use a knife.

But it was hard to keep going. There were many dark days in my life around then. When you feel despair, it's hard to find the impetus to do little things for yourself like keep your house in a good state, exercise and eat well. I ate takeaways. I was putting on a lot of weight. My life was in a steep downward spiral. Because I was quite a fun guy in public, I had to keep that pretence up, of being lively and joking and laughing, but I never enjoyed the day. Most of the times, my house was in blackness.

The only thing that helped me to keep going was the fact that I had to go and teach Taekwondo. Taekwondo inspired me to get out of my bed. But after I got home from teaching, I generally went back to bed and slept right through the day.

LOSING MY FATHER TO ALZHEIMER'S

I was so low, and the worst part of all was watching my father's condition deteriorate.

Alzheimer's is a devastating illness, and so hard for families to cope with. When I visited my father, I also had to make sure that other

"*My father was suffering.
I was suffering. I wasn't
speaking to my family. I wasn't
speaking to my mother.
I fell into a deep, deep depression*"

family members were not present due to the problems in our personal relationships. This was also a great strain.

It was so very hard for me to see my father, the one who had inspired me to become the man I am, who gave me the confidence to start my classes, found Panther Taekwondo and achieve all the things in my life that I was still so proud of – now just trapped in his own body. My father was a giant among men; he was always as fit as a fiddle. I don't recall ever even seeing him sick. It was terrible to witness his mental and physical decline.

It will never be possible to know this for sure, but I do attribute the first stroke he had to the court case against me and the problems in the family. Everyone was deeply affected and it seems more than coincidental that this happened to him at this time.

My father was suffering. I was suffering. I wasn't speaking to my family. I wasn't speaking to my mother. I fell into a deep, deep depression.

It was at this time that I started a small security firm which was called Panther Security. This meant that I was able to do night work, which allowed me time to focus on Taekwondo teaching during the day. It was very tiring but it meant that I was able to support my income, which of course had been seriously diminished by everything that had happened. Although I was exhausted, by doing two jobs I managed to keep going for a while. Finally, in 1998, came the court case.

THE CASE COMES TO COURT

I pleaded not guilty. And I was found not guilty of grievous body harm. However, I was found guilty, with a plea bargain, of a crime called affray. I had been advised that pleading guilty to the charge of affray was the best way to get the minimum sentence.

To plead 'not guilty' to any charge, my lawyer said, would be to show 'lack of remorse'. This seemed like a terrible position to be placed in when I wanted to defend my good name and fight to be cleared of all charges, but to do so might have far worse consequences.

"I felt that the situation I had been placed in was giving me an understanding of what slave labour was all about"

It wasn't a great result. But at least the terrible black cloud of dread had been lifted from me. I felt that I could get back to what I'm good at, teaching martial arts.

How wrong I was.

I was given 100 hours community service. To my embarrassment, the probation officer who was in charge of my community service, was an old school friend of mine.

And so for weeks after weeks, I had to go into people's houses and do menial work, digging gardens and cleaning out sheds. In one place we went to, the stench in the place was so bad that it made me throw up. I had to break pieces of board and move them from one side of a yard to another... that's the job I remember the most, because that was really demeaning work. What made the situation even worse was my sense of injustice. It was so hard to put this aside.

I felt that the situation I had been placed in was giving me an understanding of what slave labour was all about, not just to wear people out physically, but to reduce their sense of self-worth lower and lower. I felt like a slave. I'll never forget the day I was working in someone's garden, and a friend of mine drove past me and reversed the car back to make sure that it was me, then asked me if I'd got a new job doing labouring. I'll never forget how embarrassing it was.

I remember trying to reconcile my obligation to do community service in the daytime with the pride and pleasure I took in teaching Taekwondo in the evening. Once again I was struggling with that awful feeling of darkness hanging around me.

Although by now, my classes were beginning to grow again, fate had more pieces of ill-fortune in store for me.

On the last day of my community service, I was finishing up my work when I heard a loud bang. When I looked down the road, my car was on its side. Two lads who had stolen a car had run into the side of my

"But gradually from this low point, my life started to turn around"

car and rolled it over. They were injured and my car was smashed up. Police were all around the place. Of course, the young driver and his companion weren't insured. I didn't get any money.

At that point in my life, I had no money to fix the car. From then on, I'd be walking to my classes.

MY LIFE BEGAN TO TURN AROUND

But gradually from this low point, my life started to turn around. My classes grew to a greater size. Students who had stayed loyal to me got higher and higher up the grades, and they became black belts. They started to help me run the class, and our championship winning ways were back again.

When I'd made enough money to manage the rent, we moved to another venue in Catford, a prestigious location called St. Dunstan's College. We were there for a few years and the class grew from strength to strength. In that time, I won quite a few awards and travelled internationally with martial arts.

In 2004 we were invited to participate in a tournament in Korea, and it was while we were there that the terrible events of 1995 – now nearly ten years earlier – cast their shadow over my life once again.

While I was away at the tournament in Korea, a disaffected student had spoken to the team at St Dunstan's and given an account of what had happened which was extremely negative for me. On my return, the college bursar invited me into his office and basically asked me to leave. Once again, I'd been character-assassinated.

So we left and the re-building process started yet again.

DEALING WITH GRIEF AND LOSS

Two years after my father died, I also lost my sister. Hers was another serious loss for my family, and deeply affected my mother.

*"My mum was very proactive
in support of her daughter,
and managed to arrange her
accommodation for her in
Chelsea Pensioners' Army Barracks"*

My sister had been in the army and was living in Germany, where she had developed a problem with alcohol. My mum asked me if I could travel to Germany to rescue her from an increasingly difficult situation. I almost had to do an intervention to get her on the plane. Then an awful flight home followed, during which my sister was demanding a drink and I was determined to keep her away from alcohol so that the painful process of drying out could continue.

My mum was very proactive in support of her daughter, and managed to arrange her accommodation for her in Chelsea Pensioners' Army Barracks, as she was a services veteran. The barracks had only just opened its doors to women at that time. My mum believed, in a time before the effects of trauma and Post Traumatic Stress were understood in the way that they are now, that my sister's army experiences had a great deal to do with her problems with alcohol and that she needed support, not condemnation.

She began to receive that support, but by now she was seriously ill. She had developed diabetes along with her alcoholism, and shortly after going to live at Chelsea Barracks, she died in her sleep.

I remember going to the hospital after she died. I had been distressed by seeing my father after his death, and this made me hesitate to see my sister's body, but I felt that I should do so. When I did, I found great peace in it and was glad I had done so. She looked just as if she were sleeping.

So now my mum had survived the death of her husband and the death of her daughter. I was coping with my own grief for them, and it was hard, but I was conscious of how deeply and terribly bereaved my mother now was – and along with all of that, she was conscious of my depression and the difficulties I had had with my life and work. I was beginning to realise just what a strong woman she really was.

So I asked her: how do you manage this? How have you survived the deaths of this people who were so precious to you? It was then that

"Now, here's some personal advice that's based on very personal experience"

she told me that she had cancer too: she'd been diagnosed some time before and said nothing to the rest of the family, because she wanted to protect us.

I felt deep awe for my mum when I heard this, and how incredibly lucky I was to have had a role model like her.

She said she was determined to fight the cancer, and she did so, and seemed to be making a good recovery. Then she was told that it had spread and that now she had liver cancer, which is a serious form. I asked again if she wanted to fight.

This time she said only, *"I'm tired"*.

She was offered palliative care, and we knew that this amazing woman was not going to be with us for much longer. After my mother died, I grieved deeply. But I had learned by now, though, to contain personal sadness, as my inner discipline and strength increased.

So although I was very sad, I was able to separate those feelings from the work I needed to do.

MY OWN EXPERIENCE OF CANCER

Now, here's some personal advice that's based on *very* personal experience.

In just the same way as women should do breast checks and have cervical smear tests, men should check their testicles. Right about this time, I checked mine, and I felt something that I didn't think should be there.

I went to the doctor and was told that I needed surgery. This was during my mother's illness, and I remembered how she'd concealed it for months to protect members of her family. I decided to find the strength to do the same. I only told my brother, my wife and the vice president of Panther Taekwondo, and said to them that under no circumstances

"I decided not to let fear take over"

should word of my illness spread any further. Of course, they kept their word. I wanted my mum to be the focus of attention at this time, not me.

I reckoned without my mum, though; she was a very perceptive woman and I think she knew that something was going on. When I visited her, she'd ask me what was the matter, or if I was in pain, but I didn't want to tell her.

In the end, typically selfless and thinking about other members of her family and not about herself, my mum arranged for me to get counselling. I'll never know if she knew I was ill too, or if she just thought that I needed help and support with her cancer.

But I didn't want my mum to die thinking that I might die too. She had already grieved for one child. And I believe that we managed to achieve this for her.

I knew the inevitable ending of her illness and we were able to talk through the details and plan how she would want her funeral and commemoration to be. She was brave and dignified and we were able to do everything exactly as she had wished.

Then, at the funeral, looking down at the coffin as I gave her eulogy, I remember thinking very clearly: this could be me if my problem isn't corrected. I need to focus on my treatment and recovery.

I thought to myself quite clearly – no, I'm not joining you mum, not for quite a while.

I decided that I was going to fight the cancer, or 'The Thing' as I called it, very hard, but not allow it to become my whole reality or to dominate my life. That would mean letting fear take over. It was not going to happen.

My mum died and I went back into training and through my cancer treatment, focussing on hard work and all that I wanted to achieve in

"We've been down to nothing, overcome those challenges and grown strong again"

the future. When the surgery and treatment were over, I was offered a prosthetic testicle and said no: after all, I don't wear budgie smugglers and my wife loves me just the way I am! I said this to doctor and she laughed.

Waiting for the outcome of cancer treatment is very hard. But when the news came, it was good. My cancer had been completely removed and was unlikely to recur.

LEARNING LESSONS

By now, Panther Taekwondo Black Belt Academy had a new home, a community centre in Catford. What this building lacked in status was more than made up for by the community spirit of the place. The people who ran it were very gracious to let us use it, and we wanted to repay them by making the business thrive there. So in that location we grew one of the strongest classes in Panther Taekwondo.

That class grew exponentially; it went from strength to strength. It was at that community centre in Catford that Panther Taekwondo became what it is today.

Today, the classes have grown beyond my wildest dreams, from four to 200, from 200 to 400. We've been down to nothing more than once. But each time, we've overcome those challenges and grown back up again.

Right now I've got 800 students in 18 venues. I'm proud of my achievements and I know that Panther Taekwondo is still growing and will leave a great legacy.

FACING RACISM & DEALING WITH PERSONAL BITTERNESS

The five principles of Taekwondo have been a source of strength and guidance for me at the most difficult times of my life.

"Blaming and dwelling on grievances is a road to nowhere"

It's important to accept that other people are where they are and that their personal journey is what it is. That's showing them **courtesy.** You can't always understand why they do what they do or what their reasons are, or the way things look to them from their perspective. Most people are doing what they feel they need to do to get by and sometimes you might be the person who takes a fall as a result of that.

Integrity helps a person behave with consistency – and it does get noticed. At times in my life when I've had difficulties with my reputation or when certain allegations have been made against me, I believe that the way I have always tried to display personal integrity has helped me. It's meant that friends and supporters could see what I was about and what Panther Taekwondo is about, and they've wanted to stay with me.

Perseverance is the quality that's kept me going. Sometimes I didn't quite know how; later, I could feel that I'd learned valuable lessons about keeping going and not giving up. The ability to persevere is like training a muscle; it gets stronger and can take more pressure being applied to it. The more you persevere, the more able you are to persevere.

Self-control: there have been times in my life where I could have been overwhelmed by bitterness and anger. It's tempting, but blaming and dwelling on grievances is a road to nowhere. Self-control helps us to manage our most difficult feelings and not just vent on the people around us or look for someone to blame.

Above all, in the face of setbacks, I have many times drawn on the Taekwondo principle of *'indomitable spirit'*. In big things and in small things, it's very important to never give up – but indomitable spirit means more than that. It means believing in yourself and in the possibility of turning a situation round, even when things are very difficult and it's hard to know what the answers might be. If you give up mentally, if you start to feel hopeless inside – the way forward won't be visible to you. Indomitable spirit is about continuing to have hope and positivity. When you have that mental attitude, things become possible for you which would not have been possible otherwise.

WORKING IN TELEVISION

In 1989 I was asked to provide television commentary for the World Games and World Taekwondo Championships. In 2007, I commentated for Eurosport at the Beijing WTF World Taekwondo Championships.

GIVING BACK TO THE COMMUNITY

In 1992 I received a Metropolitan Police Commendation award, for services to the community, especially with its youth, awarded by the Chief Superintendent of Lewisham Police. In 2016 my work was also acknowledged by Ealing Police.

From 1990 until the present day I have worked as an International Taekwondo Examiner

Between 1990 and 1998 I was awarded Combat World Taekwondo Federation Man of the Year

In 1991, 1997-1999 I was Winner of the Combat Martial Arts Hall of Fame Award

1992: Winner of the Metropolitan Police Commendation Award

1993-1999: I was self-defence advisor to Lewisham and Greenwich Security Services

Panther Taekwondo Black Belt Academy has afforded local police the chance to engage with young people and also with their parents – and sometimes the chance to raise difficult issues in a community setting. In the past there has sometimes been mistrust on both sides, but I want to address these historical issues and allow young people to see the police as human beings in uniform, not as uniforms with no connection to them.

We've helped to run bullying prevention seminars as well as offering genuine empowerment to young people through teaching personal safety skills and self defence. Panther staff have also stepped in at times outside the class to prevent situations escalating and to deal with community tensions.

"People with big visions can change the world"

Dedication to community welfare and commitment to engaging with police improves youth safety in the borough of Lewisham, where we are based. This is an important foundation for young lives to be built on, and part of my desire and personal mission to make London the safest global city.

It's a big vision to have, but I don't believe that should put anyone off. People with big visions and ideas who work hard to deliver them can change the world. I want to give back to my community– it's by beginning with the people around us that we all play a part in making the world a better, safer, stronger place.

PART TWO: LEARNING

CHAPTER THREE:
GROW UP KICKING: TAEKWONDO FOR YOUNG PEOPLE

Courtesy

Integrity

Perseverance

Self-control

Indomitable spirit

These five pillars of Taekwondo can set young people up for life.

Everyone likes to feel that they've made a difference – and I'm certainly no different. In fact, I'm incredibly lucky because so many times I get to see the difference I've made. In my work as a coach, trainer and mentor to children and young people, I've seen the transformative effect of putting these five elements into practise in their lives. And each time has been just as inspiring as the first.

These five qualities that Taekwondo seeks to embody and to teach all its practitioners of any age are guidelines for excellent decision-making and then for excellent life actions. I truly believe that they are transformative – because I've seen them in action, time after time.

When we live our lives according to these principles, we see real change. We start becoming the people we've always wanted to be, and making a real, positive difference in the world around us. I don't think there's ever been a time when these five principles of thought and action have been more vital than right now.

"Everyone has different learning curves"

And it's never too early to start!

KIDS' HEALTH AND FITNESS

A lot of parents these days worry about their children's fitness and health, but it's harder than it's ever been to support their physical activity. Parents are busy, often working long hours. With traffic an ever-present worry, kids can't just play in the street. And with increasing pressure on housing in our cities, not everyone has easy access to outdoor space.

Panther Taekwondo is all about mind and body working together, and both need to be trained. Right from the beginning of a class, our warm-up is very scientific and works from head to toes: the equivalent of a traditional aerobics class in 10-15 mins (and that's before the lesson has really started!).

We work on developing a child's indomitable spirit and their will to carry on. We always push them and encourage them to try a little bit harder and to go a little further than they think they can go. We are very much aware, however, of differentiation between abilities: not everyone starts off at the same level and not everyone's physical capacity is the same. Everyone has different learning curves, and we develop each child's fitness and fighting ability along the curve that's right for them.

Whatever your starting point, physical fitness targets rise with each level of achievement in Taekwondo. We value fitness, and the self-discipline this represents. Being a great fighter is not just about doing the impressive-looking things, like the kicks or the entertaining moves, but about physical effort behind the scenes. Doing the groundwork is a vital lesson to building success.

The result of this approach is that everyone gets fitter, because fitness is the normal, healthy state for all children.

Parents agree at the start of a class that their children will be pushed quite hard. This goes against cautious attitudes you quite often hear expressed, but I find parents are supportive. This is how I know how

"We use nutrition as motivation"

many of them have serious concerns about children's fitness and health and are looking to do something about it!

We ask parents what they want from the class, and they ask us how they can help their children along. Discipline is always number one – and right behind it comes fitness. Next comes focus – and improvements in fitness are very much part of this, because mind and body work together and affect each other.

EAT WELL TO FIGHT WELL

To be fitter, you need to take care of your body, and that's why we tackle the issue of nutrition as part of becoming a better fighter. We think that education around nutrition is already good: children know what bad food is and that they should limit their intake of sweets, fried food and so on. The problem is that knowing all this isn't the same as having the motivation to do anything about it.

That's where Panther Taekwondo is a great motivator. By setting small, achievable goals for every student, we help people move forward. We find that making a start and feeling the difference takes people to a completely different level. Once you make a start, and feel you can do great things, the motivation to try harder comes automatically.

So we supply nutritional advice in all our classes, keeping it general and never specific so that no child ever feels picked on.

The other thing we find is that children are as smart as adults: they always want to know *why*. We think that's perfectly reasonable: after all, as an adult, you wouldn't follow random instructions that made little sense to you. So we give children reasons to make good choices about nutrition and health. We use nutrition as motivation. When we say to them *'don't eat sweets'*, we give them a reason: the detrimental effect that not fuelling their bodies properly will have on their ability to fight.

Close to tournaments, it's boot camp time! Parents are given an information sheet about how to best help and support their children

as they train, including the dos and don'ts of healthy eating. Newer parents sometimes hesitate to enforce this, but more experienced parents reassure them. I've even heard people say of their child: 'he tells me he doesn't want any sugar'.

Mental agility, food intake and rest are a huge part of being a successful athlete. Technical ability is important too – but it's not as important as those basic building blocks. If the basics are in place, technique can be learned. But on the most fundamental level, you are what you eat.

THE POWER OF YES

Working for a positive reward is a basic part of human motivation: I do it, you do it, everyone does it. And I think we ought to encourage that way of thinking in children too.

Too often, I believe adults have a mindset of 'no!' They're teaching children that it's bad to ask, it's bad to want, and that sense in children of wanting and aspiring shouldn't be something we encourage. But I think there's a risk when children keep hearing 'no'. Instead of learning the lesson we intend for them, we just give them a lot of discouragement.

I believe in doing the opposite; in giving them encouragement. I think we should take every opportunity to say 'yes!' – but link it to the positive action you want the child or the young person to take. We should encourage children; we should tell them that *they can.*

So when we hear: *"mom, dad, can I have a bike? Can I have this, can I have that?"*, for me the first answer should be, *"yes, if you do this".*

You can have a new bike if you get on with your homework and finish it every day and get good results in school. If you do well, you can have the thing you really want. Working hard for it will teach you its value. You're learning that you need to strive for the things you'd like, but that they aren't beyond your grasp. You can earn them with hard work. That's an immensely valuable life lesson.

"I encourage children just to feel great about themselves"

'*Yes*' should be the answer, as many times as possible. I think children need to be encouraged, and the word '*yes*' should be used more. I try and do that as much as I can in my classes and I've seen the difference it makes.

TEACHING CONFIDENCE: YOU COULD BE TEN TIMES CHAMPION

The five ways Panther Taekwondo builds confidence:

- Positive reinforcement: our staff only practice positive reinforcement with our students.

- Belt ceremony: when students advance in rank, they will become more confident by achieving their goal.

- Techniques: when starting out, students learn basic techniques that build confidence. As they advance, the techniques become more difficult but are able to be learned. As children perfect more difficult techniques, they gain confidence from their accomplishments.

- Classroom motivation: our job as teachers is to motivate and inspire. This is done in every class.

- Weekly quote: confidence is taught and explained in every class. Our weekly quote also teaches students about life skills, including confidence.

I encourage children just to feel great about themselves. I'll give you an example. There's one young chap in a class who said to me, *"sir, you were nine times British champion. Wow! Can I be nine times British champion?"*

I said, *"You could be ten times British champion".*

A light went on in his head. I saw it happen.

Children need – and we all need – a sense of possibility and a sense of personal power. And I've learned to help our children develop this. It's important to remember that children are present-focussed.

"Develop a positive success mentality"

WE NEED TO BUILD OUR CHILDREN UP

So if you just continue training them, working with them in anything, in any direction of life, and you don't give them a star, you don't give them something to aim for, you don't give them a new belt – a way of seeing and knowing that they have progressed and achieved and done well – if all they hear from us is what they did wrong and how they fell short and all the ways they didn't measure up... they'll slowly get bored and fed up, or just plain discouraged, and they'll want to do something else.

To stop that happening, when they achieve something, you have to really give them the glory for that. You have to build them up. You have to give them high fives. You have to give them some sort of certification.

That is so important for a child and for any human being. We are all like this. You have to remember when you watch the Oscars on television that these are grown-up people who go along to the prize-giving. They're grown, and they sit there waiting to see if they've been chosen. They want to see that they're recognised for their hard work, because making a film is not easy, however glamorous it looks in that moment. Behind the scenes it's hard work, and they want to be rewarded.

And here's the interesting part. *No-one tells those actors, those grown-ups, that they shouldn't feel that way, or that making the film in itself should be enough.*

Most of us find it exciting to watch other people succeed. Then, when it comes to parenting, we forget about it, or we imagine that focussing on praise will spoil our children when really the opposite is the case. We need to help children develop a positive 'success mentality' – and hearing criticism of all the things they did wrong won't motivate them to try harder and do better. That's not how it works.

Children need to be recognised. They need to be applauded when they do well. I would even say that sometimes you need to ignore their bad behaviour. In other words, you don't pay too much attention to that. That's not where the focus needs to be.

*"Many parents only interact
with their child when
they're doing wrong"*

Don't let them see that they've affected you with the bad behaviour, but applaud them when they do well. Do that, and sooner or later, they'll do well all the time. It's a natural thing, a healthy progression: it's how our minds work.

Where things can go wrong for children and young people is if they feel that they are surrounded by nay-sayers. I think children need to be rewarded for good things.

So if you're a parent, think about the interactions you have with your child and how many of those are based around negativity and the word 'no'. So many parents only interact with their child when they're doing wrong. They should interact with them when they're doing right as well.

When they do a great thing, tell them they're great, and they'll aspire to do more. Recognition and promotion and documentation saying that 'you're doing well' are great things. That's how we unleash the power of 'yes' in young people's lives.

This is why children in our classes are given small, obtainable goals. Every three months, they do a testing, and they can move up the ranks. They can appreciate that they're growing in the martial arts, and so can their parents. They can feel rewarded and know that the good they've done has been marked and celebrated.

WORKING WITH PARENTS

Right from the beginning, we involve parents in their children's learning of martial arts. Kids do best when their parents are supportive and on-side, but we also understand that sometimes parents aren't sure how best to help. We want to build confidence both ways.

All children starting their Panther Taekwondo training should make sure to practice the following basics, stances, and life skills in order to prepare for a regular training schedule.

Panther Taekwondo Stances

Stance	Description	Key tips for parents
Sparring stance (Confidence)	Student step back with right foot, feet slightly more than shoulder width apart.	1. Practice with your child and make sure he or she can step back on command. 2. This stance develops confidence over time and practice. Make sure to provide positive feedback.
Relax stance (self discipline)	Student stands up straight with hands behind back, chin up looking focused and confident.	1. Make sure your child is looking straight ahead, not fidgeting or moving body. 2. This stance develops self discipline and good posture.
Attention stance (concentration)	Student slaps hands and feet together and says "Sir". No moving and should have look of a champion.	Test your child to make sure he or she has clenched fist pushed straight down and feet together strong and says, "Sir/Miss," with a confident tone.
Kneeling position 1 (Listening skills)	Student will go down on right knee and say, "Sir," to show focus and listening skills. Both hands should also be on the left knee.	When student is on his or her knee, his or her back should be erect, and he or she should be listening with eyes on instructor.

"This is the single most important punch in Panther Taekwondo"

Panther Taekwondo Basics

Stance	Description	Key tips for parents
Middle section punch (confidence and speed)	The left fist is pulled back straight to the hip as the right fist is pushed forward until the arm is fully extended. Palm up at the moment of impact, the fist is twisted so the palm facing the ground.	1. Working on focus targets together with your child is recommended 2. This is the single most important punch in Panther Taekwondo.
High section block (timing and power)	Arms with the dominant hand the instant an opponent leads with his opposite hand. The blow crosses over the leading arm, hence its name.	1. Working on focus targets together with your child is recommended 2. After the cross is thrown, the hand is retracted quickly and the guard position resumed.
Front kick (basics and chamber)	This kick is used in both karate and kick-boxing, and students should chamber knee and then extend either kicking with ball or heel.	Parents should look into kicking shield to help student condition and practice this technique on a regular basis. This kick can be used defensively and offensively when students learn how to spar. Make sure to stretch before practicing any kicks.

"Hip rotation and power"

Roundhouse (hip rotation and power)	The roundhouse kick is when the student swings his or her leg around in a semicircular motion, striking with the front of the leg or foot.	Parents should look into a kicking shield to help student condition and practice this technique on a regular basis. Make sure to stretch before practicing any kicks.

"The real world is full of challenges"

Life Skills through Panther Taekwondo Black Belt Academy

Life skill	How we teach it	How parents can help
Leadership training	*Leadership training is taught in every class. Working with others, respecting others, and weekly assignments in class are part of our leadership training for kids.*	*Do not compare Panther Taekwondo to soccer and other team sports. Panther Taekwondo is an individual journey to greatness.* *By actively participating in leadership training camps, exercises, and other events. Invest in your child now, before it's too late.*
Work ethic	*The real world is full of challenges. We train our students that quitting is not an option. Work ethic is taught in classes and every belt rank when requirements become more difficult. Taking pride in all areas of life is taught in everyday training.*	*Do not give into your children when they want to quit or use the 'I'm bored' excuse. Make your child learn that when you set a goal you finish it.* *To help your child to not be like the rest of society and go backwards, show him or her forward thinking starts with working hard day in and day out. Let him or her know that hard work must become a habit in life for success.*

"Community involvement"

Personal growth	School teaches subjects like maths and science. Panther Taekwondo teach how to grow as a person. In classes children are taught to grow everyday, by learning from mistakes, moving forward and learning each time they make one.	1. You can make sure your child fills out a monthly personal growth checklist provided by instructor. 2. You can make sure your child is reading what is recommended by instructors.
Community Involvement	By participating in monthly community events for local charities, community groups and associations students learn to give back to their community.	1. Have your child participate in our monthly community projects. 2. By participating with your child in our monthly community projects. Lead by example for the children of tomorrow.

"Never compare your child to anyone else"

And we provide a 'parent cheat sheet': a guide to a few things that might happen as their child settles into training.

1. Students will give you a hard time when the weather is nice and friends are outside. Do not give in. If you do, they will break their habit of going to class consistently and lose focus.

2. Unless you're away for the whole summer, don't take a long summer break from classes. We only stop for one week. Our Back to School Edge Program is one of the most important components of our program.

3. When your child does not get a stripe during grading week, make sure to tell him or her that sometimes you have to work harder to get things in life. We require our students to give 100% and anything less will not earn a grading pass.

4. Never compare your child to anyone else. Everyone is here for a different reason; that is the best thing about Panther Taekwondo. If you see a student that you feel is not at the same level as your child, please understand that all students are on a personal journey to black belt. Some students may have challenges that may not be visible and they will not be discussed with someone else's parents.

5. There may be times when your child may want to quit. If this happens, use our three-step process for this.

   1. Set your child up for 2 booster classes immediately.

   2. If the classes do not work, set up a meeting where we review his or her initial reasons for joining.

   3. Attend a meeting with his/her instructors to talk about the effects of quitting.

"IF YOU SAY YOU CAN, YOU WILL. IF YOU SAY YOU CAN'T, YOU'RE RIGHT"

INDOMITABLE SPIRIT

When you experience big knockbacks, it's easy to lose confidence and to implode. It's only having a fundamentally strong attitude that can get you through that.

That's why teaching attitude to my students is the most important thing – teaching the ability to never give up. We call it 'indomitable spirit'. What it means is the will to carry on against seemingly undefeatable odds.

If water wants to break its way through rock, it continues to drip, drip, drip. So indomitable spirit means a will to carry on against seemingly undefeatable odds. Nothing is impossible to will and mind. Never say die, never say lose. Think positive.

I tell my students this all the time. They believe it. We encourage the students never to give up. That's a prerequisite when they join the class. I encourage children just to feel great about themselves and their abilities, and to have a sense that they can move forward without limitations.

The indomitable spirit, the will to carry on and to never give up, is something I've learned and I've seen it in action as I've grown my classes. I've seen it happen and I've seen the difference it makes. I've experienced it myself too. I've had that belief myself when I fought in tournaments and became British champion nine times over.

The way you begin everything, from the start of each day to starting a new school to a new project at work, is all-important. The way you begin creates the state of mind you'll perform in. We encourage our students with this mantra we use, *"if you say you can, you will; if you say you can't, you're right"*. We always encourage the children to do that, and to keep going.

RESPECT AND DISCIPLINE

Two things that come across very clearly in all my classes are discipline and respect. The important thing about respect that people sometimes

"Respect is a two way process:
you get it and you give it"

miss out is how vital it is to show it to other people, rather than just expecting them to show it to you. Respect is a two-way process.

These two qualities bring preparedness for life, inwardly and outwardly. Life's not easy, so expecting children and young people to master difficult skills isn't a bad thing for them – it's just the opposite. When they learn they can do a difficult thing, they see themselves differently from then on, as a successful person and an achiever. Giving praise for mastery of a new skill in Panther Taekwondo gives students that picture of themselves. With self-respect and discipline will come success.

It also feels good to succeed – that's why people who've had that good feeling want to have it again and will then go and work for it. The feeling of success, of being capable, comes first. Then a positive spiral of achievement gets started.

If people only hear criticism, and a list of their faults and mistakes, that inner positivity never has the chance to get started. Yet it's that which will create the strength and confidence to face the changes and uncertainties that everyone will face in life.

In Panther Taekwondo we also have a very clear definition of 'respect'. It's not just something you should get, but also something that you should give. Students understand that in order to command respect, one must both show respect to others and have respect for oneself.

And we think that repetition is very valuable. Sometimes a new lesson or understanding takes time, and it's over time that beneficial values sink into the subconscious mind where they remain as a strength to draw on for the future. It takes discipline to succeed – you have to try and try, and then you might have to try again. So we emphasise certain lessons and skills, and keep emphasising them. If we persist in telling you, you'll have the persistence to keep trying.

I've been fortunate enough to meet many inspirational children and young people and play a part in their stories of growth, journeying to maturity and achievement.

"In a chaotic world, create inner order through self-control"

FEEL LIKE A WINNER, ACT LIKE A WINNER

Panther Taekwondo insists on a respectful attitude in all its classes. Students are encouraged to contribute, and to answer questions and put questions of their own, but at the right time and in the right way. Self-respect and respect for others are inseparable.

When students learn self-control (which can take a few attempts!) they notice that they are listened to and that their words have much more effect than when they just let their enthusiasm run riot and make lots of noise. It can take time and repeated attempts to learn the confidence to hold back and find the right moment to use your strengths in a controlled way. When the outside world is disorderly and unpredictable, as it so often is, the ability to create inner order through self-control and focus becomes a powerful asset.

Being in a structured environment is likewise challenging, but students rise to it. Working as a team, supporting each other, taking turns and thinking of the dynamics of the whole situation rather than just doing what you want to do from moment to moment are all emphasised.

This is accountability, and it's how strong teams are built, as awareness of others – 'courtesy' – combines with inner confidence and self-reliance. All around are teachers and other more advanced students to act as role models for this new Panther Taekwondo skill-set.

The early days can be difficult and what makes all the difference is a positive atmosphere. Rather than 'tellings off', each Panther Taekwondo student is watched closely and their progress is encouraged.

For children and young people who have found themselves on the 'negative' side of authority before – always hearing about everything they are doing wrong – it can be transformative to realise that they are supported and to find that they are winning praise and making real progress.

Being set a difficult task – to achieve a physical fitness challenge or master a new fighting technique – is also a very positive experience.

*"To compete effectively,
you must want to win"*

Things shouldn't be too easy... because life's not easy. Learning that you *can* do it, but not necessarily at the first or second attempt, equips Taekwondo students for life as they learn the two attitudes of perseverance and *'indomitable spirit'*, then take these outside the dojo and into their everyday lives.

LIFE IS A COMPETITION

Sometimes in the modern world, we try to protect children and young people from competition. In the end, does that help them? I don't think so.

Out there in life, things are tough. They're going to have to please their bosses, their managers. They're going to have to compete with others. And to compete strongly and effectively, they need to want to win.

I don't believe (I know right now that the opinion I am expressing is not a fashionable one, but I don't need to be fashionable) that it's just about the competing and that everyone should get a prize for trying. That's not a good lesson to learn.

You have to learn to compete, and to prove your qualities. That means learning what it feels like to lose, and learning what it feels like to win, too. Then, with those experiences behind you, you can cope with both.

And in the end, it is about the winning. Children should have to compete. LIFE IS A COMPETITION. You don't just give everyone a 'C' grade. Some people get Bs and some have what it takes to get As. We should encourage our children to believe and to strive for those As.

OLIVER – IS HE OUR FUTURE PRIME MINISTER?

Oliver's mother knew that he was a bright, enthusiastic and lively child. She was very proud of his energy and persistence and the way he threw himself into everything he did. Her worry was that there was a bit too much throwing and not enough careful thinking about exactly what it was that he was trying to do!

She felt that structure was something that would really benefit him, and at first tried him in a karate class. She thought it was helpful 'but a bit disorganised', and she sensed that Oliver would benefit from really being shown how to focus.

Oliver had always been a clever and popular boy, never in any trouble... except that he just couldn't stop talking! This was the one point which was raised at every parents' evening she had ever been to. His teachers told her that Oliver talked to other people because he wanted to help them – and he certainly wasn't deliberately disruptive – but he ended up distracting the other children and getting into trouble.

He had great instincts about communicating with others. What he needed was self-control, and a chance to learn when and how to use it. Offering your words to others is something that has to be done at the right time and in the right way.

When Oliver started to learn Panther Taekwondo, he quickly began to love the sport and – slightly to his mother's surprise – he enjoyed the structure and discipline the classes provided. His mother realised that he welcomed this, and as he learned to focus he became calmer and stronger.

That's when she saw that not only would Taekwondo keep him safe, it would also teach him the right attitude about how and when to use the communication skills his teachers all agreed that he had.

"It seemed to me that this was something that was about discipline and respect for yourself and for others, and I could see that Oliver needed this. But actually", she continues, *"Taekwondo has given him so much more"*.

In Panther Taekwondo, each student quickly realises that as well as being part of a team, they matter as an individual. Oliver's mother relates how she was contacted by Ewan when she first signed Oliver up to Panther Taekwondo, asking what issues she thought would be the most important in teaching her son. *'I was very impressed with his proactivity!'* she says.

"I was very impressed with his proactivity!"

OTHER CHILDREN SENSE HIS INTEGRITY

Looking at his experiences since starting to learn Taekwondo, *"I can honestly say"*, she continues, *"that we haven't looked back! Oliver was made a prefect then later became Head Boy at his primary school. He's a school councillor; now that he can control himself and talk about the right time and in the right way, his ability to reach out to others with confidence has become an asset to him and not a disadvantage.*

"He's also a cyber-mentor; this means that he's involved in campaigns in his school to eliminate online bullying. He was chosen for this role because he's become someone that other children can readily talk to if they have concerns; they know that he'll listen to them as well as talk. They sense his integrity and feel certain that he'll respect what they tell him and make good judgements.

"And there's more. Talking confidently is an important skill for success in work and life, and this is where Oliver's greatest strengths lie. Now he can use his skills to the full, he has won two London Borough of Ealing public speaking awards. He also did very well in his SATS. He has completely stopped getting into trouble; it's as if all the energy he had before has been channelled so that he can use it to best effect instead of in an uncontrolled way. He's becoming a kind, tolerant and clever young man.

"Next year he goes to high school; he's very excited and definitely not at all nervous about taking this step. This is in no small way thanks to the confidence he has learned from Grandmaster Ewan.

"Of course, nothing is turned around by magic and Oliver has had the occasional wobble when his confidence has been knocked. But Panther Taekwondo has taught him to pick himself up, dust himself off, and never give up. He never does. He even quotes "Mum, find your indomitable spirit" to me when I've had a bad day at work! Panther Taekwondo taught him that. Most importantly, what they taught him not just the words and what they mean, but by example.

"What is the long term outcome? He will be Prime Minister one day!"

I'LL MAKE SURE YOU BECOME A BLACK BELT

Having confidence in others helps them have confidence in themselves. It's catching. At Panther Taekwondo, we believe that we decide what limits to place on ourselves… and we shouldn't place any!

So we certainly don't place them on students – we see people's future potential and the best that they have to offer, even if they've had problems before coming to the world of martial arts. Negative expectations of people are self-fulfilling, but so are positive ones and those are one we focus on – always..

In the words of black belt fourth dan Master Jonathan Registe, *"April 22nd was a very special day for two reasons. Firstly, it was my sixth birthday and I was excited at the prospect of having family at my home generously showering me with gifts. Secondly, and more importantly, this was my first day of training at Panther Taekwondo, which I had long aspired to join since watching with envy my sister train for three years.*

"My first encounter with Master Ewan was one which I'll never forget, mainly because I was so nervous and did not know what to say to him when he spoke to me. But I'll always remember what he said: "I will make sure that you become a black belt one day". That's when I knew I was in good hands. And from that moment, I really believed that there were no limits to what I could achieve. Then, as I learned that I could increase my skills in sport and become able to do things that would once have seemed unachievable, I started to see that the same thing was true in other areas of life.

"Nineteen years later, and with a black belt Fourth Dan Master Grade to my name, I am proud to say that Master Ewan indeed was correct. Even though there have been some trials and tribulations on my journey, Master Ewan has always been there to reassure me that I can be and can do whatever I want to do both in life and in Taekwondo.

"His inspiring phrases, especially 'if you say you can, you will, and if you say you can't, you're right" have become a way of life to me. It's been an inspiration. Feeling that there are people who believe in you and in your potential is the best way to learn to believe in yourself.

"I am personally passionate about working with children to stop them carrying — let alone using — knives on the street"

"Having good teachers who encouraged me so much helped me to realise that my own strengths and gifts also lie in teaching I'm now a qualified teacher working in a primary school. And I've also become a Panther Taekwondo teacher, and opened my own Panther Taekwondo school so that I can inspire youngsters like me to reach out to all the opportunities life offers in the same way that I was inspired.

"Without Master Ewan's guidance and encouragement, I doubt I would be where I am today. I feel indebted to him and to everyone at Panther Taekwondo. I'd like to say thank-you to all my teachers, but I think that making my life the best it can be and fulfilling my dreams is the best kind of thank you".

KIDS AND KNIVES

Young people face difficult challenges in life. It's easy for them to be drawn into negative patterns of behaviour, or to use as role models people who won't teach them positive things about themselves. And there's one aspect of modern life for too many young people in our cities which casts a long and frightening shadow – and that's knives.

I am personally passionate about working with children to stop them carrying – let alone using – knives on the street.

How can we change the mindset of our children? How can we stop them from being aggressive towards each other? I'm aware of gangs and rivalries between areas – but what is it that makes children believe that because they live in a certain area code, that they have to fight another person in another area code, or even mug them or take their mobile phone from them?

When I was younger, I could travel from South London to East London, from Camberwell to Peckham, without a worry. There was no area code to me. So where did this way of thinking come from?

However it started, it goes very deep and this troubles me. I asked one of the children about it one time, when the kids were hanging about at Panther Taekwondo.

"I believe that through martial arts, these divided ways of thinking can be broken down"

I said to him, *"What's this thing about area codes? Why do you protect your area so much?"*

He goes, *"yeah, well, we look after Northolt, It's our place"*. I said, *"so you're protecting Northolt. From who?"*

And he answered, *"yeah, from them guys up in Ruislip"*.

So I said, *"Is Northolt paying you to do this? Why do you have to do this?"* And he couldn't answer.

I realised it wasn't something he'd really thought about. (If he had, it might not have seemed such a good idea). It's just something that's been embedded in them.

If there's one thing that I'd love to do, it's change that mindset. I believe that through martial arts, these divided ways of thinking can be broken down. My classes are for children (and of course for adults) from many different backgrounds and cultures. Everyone learns respect. Then everyone shows it to everyone else, and suddenly you've got the beginning of real changes in attitudes that can carry forward into all areas of young people's lives.

That's why I do believe there's a chance for those guys if we could get them into martial arts or if they had a little help or support before these ways of thinking became really embedded. In our day, there were youth centres. There were places that people could go to. These days, there's nothing. Government decisions have taken those things away.

Now I don't want to get too political about this, but I do believe that if something valuable is lost, we need to look around us in society and ask what else can step up to plug that gap, and if there's another faction who could help in the future, because something valuable has been lost and if it's not replaced, there will be a cost to that.

For example, there are churches. Churches usually run on Sunday, maybe, Saturday, sometimes Friday as well. Friday, Saturday, Sunday. What do they do with that hall for the rest of the week? That's where

"People join a street crowd because they haven't got a gang already. Gang culture is surrogate family"

the children could go and have a little bit of fun and have a little interaction amongst each other. They'll get to know each other. They'll become a community. They'll stop fighting each other.

That's what we had when I was a child. In some ways, times were tough but we didn't fight each other. We didn't go looking for trouble, because we had other things to do. Sometimes, as they say, the devil finds work for idle hands. I believe that's often what's happening to the children these days, so there must be a way we can change their perceptions. It's vital – absolutely vital – to give young people a sense of purpose, and to offer them something constructive and valuable to do.

And the younger we start this, the better, before these self-destructive attitudes have a chance to take hold. If parents and people like myself, community leaders, and the police could reach young people before these attitudes have a chance to take hold, that's where the chance for a different future is.

I always remind people that the police do a very hard job. They don't know who's bad or who's good. They find out afterwards. But if all of us could work together as a community, I know that we can stop these stabbings, this senseless violence and destruction, this waste of lives that's going on. It could change.

WHO IS YOUR FRIEND?
DEVELOPING INDEPENDENT JUDGEMENT

Unfortunately, I've seen young people become involved in gang culture. Keeping them away from this is something I feel strongly about, but criticising and being negative isn't the way.

If you can see that someone is going down a wrong path, the first thing to do is to understand why.

For too many kids, this is something that's missing: a secure base, a sense of structure, people you belong with who'll always be there for you.

*"With strong self-worth,
the need to get involved in gang culture
diminishes"*

Understand that sense of lack they feel, that emptiness, and now you can start to understand how much they want to do something to fill it, and why they join gangs and follow along with what other gang members do.

I'm sad for some of these kids, and I want to keep them out of harm's way. With a sense of self-worth and a feeling of security, their need to join gangs and follow people who seem like powerful leaders but aren't a good influence would be diminished.

When you're confident in who *you* are, you see more clearly who *the gang leaders* really are, what they're really about and whether this is a good place for you to be. You can make different decisions, ones that are better and more positive for you and for the direction of your life.

Martial arts training makes you confident in yourself, deep down inside. It means you don't have a need to test yourself, or to act tough in front of others. (Acting tough often just means covering up your vulnerability). Feeling sure of yourself and able to use independent judgement means that you can take real control.

So if there's an issue arising, you can decide to either act as peacemaker, or to walk away. There's nothing for you to prove, and no insecurity you have to hide. Martial arts training enables you to choose your battles and to have to confidence not to have to prove yourself to anyone.

FEEL THAT YOUR LIFE LACKS EXCITEMENT? THEN COME TO PANTHER TAEKWONDO!

Something else young people want is excitement, challenge – the feeling of stretching themselves. And there's nothing wrong with that. But unfortunately it can be missing for too many children.

Panther Taekwondo classes give children all the excitement they could ever want.

You can shout as loud as you want – we encourage it!

*"In a Taekwondo class,
we are all one person"*

You can fight someone and not get arrested!

You can feel like a winner – because you really are one!

A class has everything you could do on the street, but the environment is controlled.

I SAY HELLO IN TWENTY DIFFERENT LANGUAGES

The only things you can't do in a Panther Taekwondo class are:

• You can't swear

• You can't be racist or sexist

• You can't be macho

We teach our students to accept everyone for what they are. All religions, races and creeds attend the classes, and all of them get on. One of the bonuses of my job is that it's always new year for someone, so there's always something to celebrate!

Our classes are wonderful melting pots, microcosms of a global society, happening right now here in England. I learn about different religions all the time. I can say 'hello' in 20 languages.

But in the class - we are all one person. Our characters and beliefs may set us apart – but there is so much more that draws us together.

ONE STUDENT'S INDOMITABLE SPIRIT

Above all else, I teach the children in my classes indomitable spirit. What that means is to never, ever give up: go under, go around, go over the top, but never give up. I could have easily given up at difficult times in my life, and if I had done so I wouldn't be where I am today.

So that's really the passion for me in the long run: to keep moving forward. Some people think because they're not moving forward fast,

then it's time to stop. It's time to stop if you're not moving forward. If you're moving forward, even slowly, keep moving forward.

If you're going to keep going in difficult times, you need to develop that persistent, indomitable attitude where you keep on trying to solve your problems and don't have a voice in your head telling you to quit or that there's no point trying or that you can't get through this. You need to believe that all your effort is going to be worth it in the end.

One former student who knows this for sure is Jenna, and here is her remarkable story.

A JOURNEY TO RECOVERY

Jenna started Panther Taekwondo classes back in 2006 when she was 11 years old. To start with, it wasn't a big decision for her, just something that she tried out because her sister was interested. However, this changed very quickly.

Something about the class really spoke to Jenna: in her own words, "I fell in love with the art of it, and with the etiquette. I quickly realised that Panther Taekwondo would become a way of life for me".

Jenna started to work very hard and passed all her gradings. She was featured in the local paper because of her success in rising up the levels of Taekwondo so quickly; on one occasion she moved up more than one level in a single grading test, which hadn't happened at Panther Taekwondo for over 21 years. She felt proud and happy.

Then, at the age of just 13, Jenna was rushed to hospital with a life-threatening infection. Starting in her hip, it spread quickly down her legs and into her vital organs, resulting in multi-organ failure. She was in a grave condition; her parents were told that her life might be in danger. Only four other people in Great Britain have suffered from this extremely rare condition.

This was a dreadful crisis for Jenna. She underwent major surgery and

*"The more I learned about Taekwondo,
the stronger
I felt myself to be"*

her family remained at her bedside.

In Jenna's own words:

"By complete co-incidence, Master Ewan Briscoe was in the same hospital as I was at the very same time (he'd suffered a slipped disc). I knew that lots of people were worried about me but I had no idea that he was there until he arrived. I was in and out of a coma but I remember hearing him speaking to me. My mother described how I stirred and raised my fist into an on-guard position. Because Taekwondo means so much to me, I found a really deep inspiration in doing this. I knew then that I would survive.

"I was in hospital for another three months, but what had happened seemed so remarkable to me that I spent that time learning the Taekwondo syllabus, concentrating not just on the physical training – as I was still stuck in bed a lot of time – but on the mental training aspects. The more I learned about Taekwondo, the stronger I felt myself to be even thought I was still in hospital and my doctors were still quite worried about my progress.

"When I was feeling stronger, they had bad news for me. I'd survived, but they told me my ability to walk had been affected by my illness. I might have to use a wheelchair for the rest of my life. As anyone would be, I was shocked and afraid. I was used to living a healthy life; now I didn't know what the future had in store for me.

"After returning home, my first thought was to visit Panther Taekwondo. I arrived in my wheelchair, then got up and walked to the front of the class using crutches. Everyone gave me a standing ovation. I was back home.

"Next, I started physiotherapy. Grandmaster Ewan made time in his schedule to help me learn to walk again. It was hard work and sometimes felt very slow, but as he said, when you're making progress, keep moving forward. Some things take time.

"And slowly, I did learn to walk properly again. Sometimes it felt like I'd lost so much ground – as if I was starting again from the beginning, having to re-learn the basics, whether that meant in Taekwondo or just taking a

"It didn't just save my life – it taught me indomitable spirit"

few steps across a room. But with lots of encouragement from Grandmaster Ewan and all my classmates, I persisted.

"At the age of 15, I successfully achieved my 1st Dan black belt. I knew from that day that Panther Taekwondo wouldn't just be a way of life for me. It was also going to be my career.

"Since then I've achieved my second, third and fourth Dan. I've starred in a YouTube documentary and become a master grade at Panther Taekwondo. I now run classes and I've been promoted to the Panther management team.

"My health problem as a result of the infection aren't over yet; I had to have hip replacement surgery and go through a long recovery process afterwards. But I'm determined to go on and achieve more.

"I honestly feel that without Panther Taekwondo, I wouldn't be here today. It didn't just save my life — it taught me indomitable spirit."

"Let's look again at the five guiding principles of Taekwondo"

CHAPTER FOUR:
THE WARRIOR IN THE WORKPLACE

Let's look again at the five guiding principles of Taekwondo. This time, we're going to apply them to life in the workplace.

These guiding principles can help you find success in your work, fulfil your professional dreams and become someone you always dreamed of being. They can help you respond to the challenges of the modern workplace and face the future with confidence.

Courtesy

Integrity

Perseverance

Self-control

Indomitable spirit

Whatever you are doing in your life to make a living, there are core attitudes we all need for success at work. These attitudes need to be at the heart of us, which means they'll be at the heart of everything we do.

Taekwondo teaches those attitudes, and its lessons can be applied to our working lives, no matter where or how you work.

DEAL WITH REALITY – EVEN IF IT'S TOUGH

The first thing we all need is the ability to face reality – even if we don't like it much at first.

"So taking risks was my choice"

I chose the difficult and challenging road of building something for myself and taking risks, back in a time when many people could still rely on a safe job, steady employment and a good pension waiting for when they retired. For many people in those days, there was a lot more certainty about the future.

So taking risks was my choice.

But now, as I look around me, I see that many people don't have a choice. More and more of us live with uncertainty about the future. Many of us today live very different lives from those of our parents and grandparents: they work for themselves, or on short contracts, or change careers several times rather than following one well-trodden path. They have to find their own way in life.

Safe jobs, safety nets and good pensions are nowhere to be seen. The workplace is tougher and more competitive. We're under increasing pressure to succeed. I don't want to get political about this: my point is that this is the new reality. When the world changes, we have to change and adapt to survive.

This is what many of us are facing. This is what our children will face. We, and they, need to be ready for it.

ACCEPT AND COPE WITH CHANGE

This rate of change isn't slowing down; it's getting faster. In the future, technology will keep transforming the world of work, and we'll need new skills and abilities to keep up with the fast pace of technological and social change..

So we need to think about preparing ourselves in a different way from the way people used to in the past. Back then, you learned a skill or a trade or a profession and it could set you up for life.

Now we need different strengths and skills from the ones our parents' generation had. We need a different mental approach too. We need to

"There's no such thing as job security"

be fast on our feet, independent-minded, resilient, adaptable, creative, confident and determined.

In my work as a trainer and mentor for people in all walks of life, I've seen the personal empowerment that can be achieved through the principles of Taekwondo, the success it leads to and the way it equips people to deal with the changes and challenges we all face. It's one of the reasons why I created Panther Taekwondo. I'm proud of the many achievements of my students and former students. It's wonderful to be part of so many exciting life journeys going to such great places.

I've seen how Panther Taekwondo brings a focus and mental discipline to practitioners' lives and helps us channel our energies in a transformative way. It's vital to be able to do this as we all have to face a future without certainties.

KEEP FLEXIBLE, STAY CREATIVE

So - there's no such thing as job security. That's the reality we have to deal with.

What we can have, though, is the security created by our own attitudes: creativity, flexibility and above all by our indomitable spirit. That means the spirit that doesn't give up, that persists and finds a way through. We can know that we will overcome whatever the set of circumstances it is that we are facing.

That's certainly something I've had to learn about and realise in myself, so now it's something I want to teach. I believe I can use the difficult experiences I have had to inspire others.

Now I'm going to be very honest here : there have been times when I thought I wasn't going to survive. A bill has come in, and I've thought: there is no way I'm going to pay this bill. Simple as that.

If you're facing something like this right now, or if you do in the future, the fact is that *you will pay*. Along the way you might lose something, or

"We were martial artists. We didn't have to look terrifying"

find that you must prioritise one thing over another thing. You might lose something that seems important to you. But you will find a way through this situation and you will go on.

Back in the days when I got bills like that falling through the letterbox, bills that seemed at first as if there was going to be no possible way to pay them, I learned to take those difficult situations one step at a time. Don't open the bill before breakfast then find that you can't eat breakfast because of stress. Eat first, take in the energy you need to cope with the situation, then you're ready to deal with it. You'll need to find a way: work a bit harder, get another job… but you can show the will to carry on against seemingly undefeatable odds.

In 1995, as I related earlier in this book, I was having a very difficult time. I'd been accused of a serious crime and as a result, student numbers at Panther had fallen very low. I had rent to pay on properties I'd been using for the school, and a mortgage to pay on my home. I had a family who depended on me. What I didn't have was the money to pay for any of these.

It was time for indomitable spirit.

That was when I founded Panther Security, working with a small group of friends with a martial arts background who I knew well. We got work, covering door security at a venue in Catford, near Lewisham, then built up from there to work at other venues after recommendations.

We used our sense of humour to get us through a crisis, and advertised ourselves as 'extraction technicians'. We said that we were gentlemen: we'd work like receptionists, not big beefy bouncers – but then if there was a problem and someone had to leave and was being aggressive… well, we were martial artists and we could cope with that. We could extract them, no trouble, because we were all about fitness, flexibility and fighting skills. We didn't have to look terrifying.

Wayne Wright and Gilbert Barnet were working with me: they were my right hand men during this difficult time. In the present day, both

"I was assigned as security guard to Seve Ballesteros"

of them run successful fitness businesses and it's great to see the success they've gone on to achieve.

The way we approached our security work was a lot more about talking than about force: we'd keep the atmosphere in a venue pleasant and deal with problems before they got serious. A lot of the time in security, situations come down to respect and community reputation. If you have that, people are civil to you even if they have a reputation as the bad boy in the area.

So we got more gigs and ended up running the business for about three years. Around the time that celebrity TV presenter Jill Dando was shot on her doorstep in Fulham, there was a high level of anxiety around and a lot of work coming in for us, sometimes providing security for well-known individuals.

We were invited to provide personal security and chauffeuring services for PGA tournaments, which was how I met some famous golfers... and ended up learning a very valuable lesson from no other than Seve Ballesteros.

THE IMPORTANCE OF THE FOLLOW THROUGH

I never thought that any of us martial arts guys would get into golf, but here's how it happened. I was assigned as security guard to Seve, and one day I was out on a green with him. I watched him as he took a swing at a ball.

It didn't look like much effort, but that ball hung in the air for ever. It seemed like it was never going to fall to earth. I was impressed.

He asked me if I'd like to have a go. I swung at the ball and made contact. The ball travelled a few feet. I tried again. Same result.

Then he asked me: 'if you're going to land a kick in Taekwondo, do you do that with your legs stiff, or with your legs flexible?' And that's when I realised that just like my sport, golf was all about doing things with

"A lot of mistakes come from having a rigid attitude"

the right technique. It might look easy – but it wasn't. It took skill and it took practice. Seve had put in the time and he had the skills.

The other thing he told me about was *follow through*. The term he used was 'sequential movement'. The sequence of making a swing in golf involves your whole body; it's a flow. It travels from your feet to your ankles to your knees to your hips and up your torso into your arms where the muscles are waiting for the swing. Then after you've connected with the ball, that movement continues in a long, smooth follow-through.

That's when I started to understand golf for the very first time. Golf is like Taekwondo, in this respect. It's about connected, sequential movement; it involves the whole body. You focus on the end result, the contact with the ball, or with the opponent, but you don't lock yourself rigid. You flow into it.

A lot of mistakes in life and work come from a very rigid attitude. We might think that we know what we are doing, but really we're afraid and that inhibits our freedom. So we are only doing a small movement when we need to do a much larger one, involving our whole body.

It takes confidence to relax into the flow. When we are tense and controlled by fear, sequential movement becomes far more difficult for us. If we can relax, go with the sequence of actions, then follow through, the result will be far more powerful.

THE POWER OF PERSISTENCE

This one is simple - it means: STICK AT IT. Over and over again, Panther Taekwondo teaches its students not give up and not to give in – to keep trying until we get the thing that it's important to us.

As Bruce Lee said: *"don't fear the fighter who knows 1001 ways to kick and can do them all quite well. Fear the fighter who's done one kick 1001 times, because that fighter has mastery"*.

"There are no shortcuts to mastery"

Back in the late 1980s, when Panther Taekwondo first had a strong community presence in the London borough of Lewisham, I was invited to give a demonstration to Royal Mail staff in the local office. As part of the display, I did a spinning kick – twisting through 180 degrees then kicking an apple balanced on somebody's head.

Afterwards, a lot of people wanted to know: *how did you do that?*

If you do something 3000 times, it becomes as natural as eating. This is one of the lessons Panther Taekwondo teaches best: the will to carry on, and the persistence and discipline to make those 3000 kicks.

For the first 1500 tries, there was no-one standing in front of me. Then for the next few hundred kicks, there was someone there but a lot of padding in place in case my kick missed. Then, when I was sure I had mastered the move and could do it without thinking about it – I did it for real, with someone's real head right there.

We used to joke about practising that move, doing it over and over again until we were sore. The joke was that our feet were frightened of apples. We even gave our problem a name: 'applefoot'. But behind the joke is serious business. There are no shortcuts, no quick tricks to get you through. There is only practice and repetition. If you want to do well, be the best, really amount to something – keep practising.

NOTHING IS IMPOSSIBLE TO A WILLING MIND

If I want to punch my way through a wall - that might sound impossible. But if I really want to get through it, bit by bit, it will weaken under my attack. Eventually bits will start to fall off that wall and cracks will appear. In the end, if I want to, I will punch it until I break through.

We demonstrate this in classes with pieces of wood, by challenging the children to break them. We always set small, attainable goals, so to start with the pieces of wood are small too. But while the children are working on breaking their first small piece, they see others students around them who can break larger ones.

"The reality of the modern world is that whatever you do, however you make your living, to some extent you are working in marketing"

When they see other children breaking the wood, they know that they will – and this shows in the questions they ask. "When will it be my turn to break the wood?' they say. They believe that success will come, so success will be a given.

A long time ago, when I was a young boy, my mother and I attended an interview with a careers adviser. He asked me what sort of work I would like to do when I was grown up. At that time I was interested in architecture and in design, and later on I did work in graphic design. I told the careers adviser that right now, what I was interested in was becoming an architect.

His response was to advise me to get a job in the post office.

My mother decided that she'd heard enough and she ended the trip to the careers adviser right then and there. She recognised racism in his response, and the placing of a limit on my sense of possibility. Whether he was conscious of it or not, that careers adviser wanted to take away my belief that I could become an architect and replace it with something smaller.

That experience has stayed with me. To this day, it always makes me respond – yes, I can.

THE POWER OF PR

The reality of the modern world is that whatever you do, however you make your living, to some extent you are working in marketing. We all are.

You're marketing yourself: to your employer if you have one, to your manager, to the people around you and to the outside world. You are building a career based on your performance and your reputation, and no-one is going to do that work for you. No-one's going to hand you the promotion, the opportunity, the next step up, on a plate. You need to make them aware of you and of what you've achieved. You need to promote what you've done – to shout your achievements from the rooftops.

"Be your brand. Be it,
look it and live it"

You have to become a brand. Then you must market your brand to the world.

BUILDING YOUR BRAND

Right from the beginning at Panther, we understood this. We knew that our reputation, the impression we made and how other people saw us was key to our success. To be the team to beat – we needed to *be seen as* the team to beat.

Back in the late 1980s, hardly any clubs used to go to Taekwondo tournaments in tracksuits. Instead, people would just turn up in their Taekwondo suits. We wanted to feel like a team and act like a team – so we decided to start by *looking* like a team.

Team colours and markers are important. They are badges of belonging; they say to you and to the people around you that you're part of something. The first year, we wore baseball caps with the Panther logo. The next year it was Panther branded track suits. Then it was smart two piece suits and dark glasses – and the parents wore dark glasses too.

Master Andy Davies said that *"it was like watching the storm troopers walk in – my mouth was open. It was like these guys had come to take over"*.

Of course, other teams responded and raised their branding game. So we responded again, always pushing ahead, one bigger, one better. Now we went for cheerleaders, in black and yellow club colours. In the best traditions of cheerleading, they even had pompoms. I'd take a ghetto blaster (this was in the days when ghetto blasters were very big and impressive-looking) and have the song that became our theme tune, Public Enemy's *Don't Believe The Hype,* playing in the background as well.

Branding is very important: it needs to be everywhere and it needs to be consistent. Whatever you decide your personal brand is to be, you need to look it and live it and be it.

"A tribute to the late, great boxer and fighter Mohammed Ali"

RAISE THE ENERGY

Two coach-loads of supporters would always come along to our tournaments, and we supplied them all with a horn so that they would blow them when our fighters went on. We were once asked to quiet our crowd! But we were up in the stratosphere: the goal was to raise our energy and keep it high. Even if was an early start on the road, we'd begin in the coach, chanting and singing – we're up, we're awake, we're going to do this.

Then we'd harness our competitive instincts and take bets: who'd deliver the quickest knockout to an opponent? Fun, friendly competition within our squad kept the energy high and everyone on their toes. Who'd do the prettiest knock-out (meaning using the most graceful and stylish technique?) We even bet on who'd wear the flashiest suit or eat the biggest packed lunch. What it was didn't matter. What mattered was us, bonding as a team.

We used chants and slogans to enthuse our supporters and inspire ourselves to perform to the very best of our ability – and beyond.

One of them was a tribute to the late, great boxer and fighter Mohammed Ali:

Float like a butterfly, sting like a bee, your foot can't kick where your eyes can't see! That meant our fighters were moving too quickly for their opponents to land kicks on them... and one thing was for sure: when they heard that chant going up from our supporters, they moved even faster!

We're tougher than tough!

We're rougher than rough!

We're lions, we kick through iron!

We even used Bob the Builder:

Can we kick it, yes we can!

This was fun and we intended it as fun, but we also use the chants during training so the fighters would get used to a sound like a mantra, inspiring them on. Then when they heard the mantra again in a tournament they could access the energy of the training session to help them fight harder.

BRANDING IS ALL ABOUT THE DETAIL

Even at tournament level, if there's a chap who's taller than me, I'll walk towards him on my toes, giving the impression and illusion of height. Next I give a firm handshake and pull him towards me – controlling the ring already. I'll bang on his shoulder with my fist – let's have a good fight – but he feels the force.

When you're building your brand, appearance matters, in big and small things. You have to stand out and be impressive. Even if not every fighter is great, the whole impression is great.

When a new prospect comes into the class I make sure I've had a manicure because I'm going to have to point things out and he or she will notice my hands. If you're showing a price list, point with a nice pen, not a chewed old biro. We travel to competitions in pristine coaches.

All our classes are structured the same way, with front desk, chairs round the side and flags of many nations in the same position so that if parents go to another class, everything is the same and they immediately recognise the Panther Taekwondo brand.

PUBLICITY MATTERS

In the world of work, no-one knows what you're doing unless you tell them you're doing it. It doesn't matter how great you are: unless you focus on your own publicity, chances are that you will be overlooked. Remember you're working in PR!

Once you've established your personal brand, it's up to you to get it out there, in the digital world and the real world too. Use social media:

Twitter and Instagram. Take every chance to be recognised for what you do. Volunteer and gain experience – put yourself forward to lead. Every experience is a chance to develop and learn.

So before we arrived at a tournament, we'd contact the local publicity and PR networks: the press, the mayor's office. We'd invite local figures to give prizes to our fighters. Our reputation for bringing good news of success in our endeavours back to Lewisham got us so well recognised that we had a base at the mayor's office!

Our main rivals were Slough Taekwondo, where Grand Master John Webster, Master Stuart Armatrading and Master Ian Willock fought. From the Manchester Olympians, there was Grand Master Mark Richardson. From Northampton, there was Master Maurice Young. These were all friendly rivalries and we inspired each other to fight harder and become better.

GLADIATORS – A REAL FIGHTING BRAND

Now we come to the very exciting lessons I learned from one of media's top fighting brands, and a few lesson I taught them myself! I was proud to work with and train two of the TV series most famous Gladiators, Cobra and Panther.

How did it happen?

STRIKING WITH COBRA

One year, TV programme makers came to the gym. They attended the class and asked if anyone was interested in a new TV show. A fighter called Michael Wilson was there that day: he was a very fit, good-looking guy who really stood out with his blond hair like Thor, the legendary Norse god. (Apart from that, though, he wasn't so much like Thor, just a very down-to-earth, funny and likeable guy).

He was picked to audition for the show, although no-one was quite sure what it was at that stage. The auditions took place at Woolwich

"For Panther, raising her game was more about fighting technique than about increasing general fitness"

Barracks, and centred around an obstacle course. Michael Wilson could certainly climb. I knew he'd do well.

And indeed he did do very well. His performance that day helped turn him into the feared TV gladiator, Cobra. As Cobra, he used lots of martial arts techniques, including Taekwondo's spinning kicks, as well as moves from Thai boxing.

Next I met Panther, the fearsome female gladiator, by a slightly different route. It was back when I did security work for the English Federation of Body Builders, who wanted martial artists on the doors for some of their events. That's how I met Panther's husband, then eventually the super-fit woman herself.

Martial arts give a fighting edge – and Panther was smart enough to know this.

I started training Panther in long sticks fighting as I could see from her TV performances that she needed better technique in this to deal with some really tricky opponents. Gradually our training became a regular thing and I used to travel to Uxbridge to train her at 7am in the morning.

For Panther, raising her game was more about fighting technique than about increasing general fitness, because she was already one of the fittest gladiators. She owned her own gym and was British bodybuilding champion. The skills of martial arts, however, can add a fighting edge to anyone and Panther was smart enough to know this.

I used to travel with Cobra, and worked in his personal security detail as well. The guy worked really hard, visiting schools and making himself super-accessible to do as many visits as possible and really get the word out to kids about health and fitness among young people. He was very keen to motivate them and encourage their knowledge of fitness, training and nutrition in schools. He used to come down to Panther Taekwondo classes and help out there too.

*"If you don't take pride
in something, why is it
worth your time?"*

As a trade-off for my work as a trainer, my students and I were offered tickets to come and watch the Gladiators show being filmed at the weekend, at least three times per series. This was so exciting for the kids... and I have to admit I got pretty excited along with them.

PRIDE AND PASSION IN YOUR WORK

There's nothing like sharing a passion for something with another person to forge strong bonds between you.

Passion for what you are doing in your life is rocket fuel. Find it and use it, and it can take you higher and further than you could ever have dreamed.

Life without that passion is duller, flatter and so much less satisfying. Your passion is something you need to find, and then ignite, to help you on your way. When it's missing, sooner or later you'll get problems.

I really dislike poor customer service. But whenever I receive it, instead of blaming the person who's done a bad job, I ask a different question. I ask why it happened. I wonder why this person is in that job in the first place.

If you take no pride in something – why is it worth your time? That's a question we should all be asking ourselves when we look at our working lives.

I encourage as many of my students as possible to take a very independent approach to their careers, and if they can, to work for themselves, or consider doing so in the future. If this doesn't work for you, or if there's a career path you're already following that's really going well for you, this independence of mind is still the key to success.

Whether or not you're in business for yourself, you're in business for yourself!

That's because your employer isn't the one who's looking out for your interests. You can't just stay in a job and know that you'll be helped on your way, or wait to make progress automatically.

"A black belt is a state of mind"

Whether or not you're in business for yourself – nowadays, you ARE in business for yourself! It's down to you to look ahead, take ownership of your career and decide where you want to go next, then talk to your employer about how this can happen. It's up to you to take that initiative. You need to own the process.

And to do that, you need to be doing the right work for you: your passion, pride and motivation need to be strong. If they're not, you'll struggle to get focused and stay focused.

One of the ways we motivate our instructors at Panther Taekwondo is that they know they can make real progress. That's one reason all our instructors have pride and passion: they know that if they work hard with me they could become management in the company. I offer a ladder to give people ownership.

It might be that in your working life, that ladder is not being offered to you. It's up to you to go and find it. That's tough – but you can still do it, using your persistence and indomitable spirit.

In the higher levels of Taekwondo, you'll find that those qualities are really developed – and you'll certainly be needing them. It takes one year of work to get from First Dan to Second Dan: that's twelve months of training, technical ability, attendance, persistence, the quality of your work and the application and mental attitude you show.

A black belt is state of mind. It's more than just a sign that you've mastered certain technical skills to a very high level – although by this time you'll certainly have done that. We have discussions with parents and teachers, asking them about the behaviour of their teenagers at home, so we know that the qualities we are looking for have taken root and are being expressed beyond the classroom.

We're looking for a child who knows that to win, he or she has to work hard and consistently. We don't need to hear that every pupil is top of the class, but we expect to hear that they want to be!

*"Whoever has the
Crown Jewels — rules!"*

We're also looking for fortitude. That's a quieter, stronger quality. We're not so interested in the class clown as the guy who's looking to govern the class clown, creating order and a respectful environment for learning.

We're looking for the right attitude to parents or carers, and to authority.

If you're living underneath your parents' roof, 'who has the Crown Jewels, rules'. That means showing respectful behaviour and being prepared to wait for rewards. Are pupils helping older relatives? Assisting around the house or with younger siblings? If your parents agree you are ready for the step up to maturity that being a black belt represents, that's great, but if you've got it in class but not at home or in school, you're going to have to wait until you've shown that you're really ready.

Of course, that means that every single person who earns black belt status at Panther Taekwondo appreciates it. That sets them up on a good course: they've learned the value of hard, consistent effort.

MONEY COMES FROM SUCCESS, SUCCESS COMES FROM PASSION

There's no way you can possibly make money unless you're doing something you're passionate about.

Money comes from success, success comes from passion - and nine times out of ten you need to work for yourself to make money. That's why I encourage my students to become self-employed, or at least if they are not, to think about themselves as free agents who must work to advance their career, rather than wait for someone to do it for them.

Unless you have a mission in life, a reason for doing what you do – you're going to struggle when times get tough to find the reason why you're working.

My first career was in graphic design and I enjoyed it. I worked for a large and well-known company and the firm was supportive of me when I wanted time off work to travel to tournaments and fight – at

*"I could see how vital it was
to be my own boss"*

first. I think they liked the prestige of employing the champion that I was becoming.

But over time, as I needed more time off to travel to tournaments, and time off to recover from inevitable injuries, they became less keen. Eventually I realised that this situation could only end one way, and decided to jump before I was pushed. After that I did more than one job, working as much as I could to raise money to open my own Taekwondo school.

I could see how vital it was to be my own boss, to be able to have time off when I needed it and not have to answer to someone else.

WHAT I LEARNED FROM THE FAST FOOD INDUSTRY

In every aspect of life is the opportunity to learn. I based my business model on something as ordinary and everyday as McDonald's, the burger chain.

Everyone starts off with the same basic training.

Everyone starts at the bottom and is told they can rise.

Shops compete with each other, just as our classes compete with each other. Classes in Panther get rewarded for being the best class, and this competition fuels friendly rivalry, raises more money for teachers and raises standards.

Master Jonathan Regis once recruited 70 students in 4 weeks; everyone else set out to recruit 71. Except for Master Jenna Gosling, our first and youngest female Fourth Dan – she decided to double the target and aim for 140. We encourage that kind of good-humoured competition – and her great attitude to winning shows exactly why she's made the progress in Taekwondo that she has.

We aim to create the same structure that a busy fast food joint has, with everyone focussed on a task and knowing exactly what they have to do, so that the product emerges consistently. It's quite regimented.

"Value your own time and respect other people's"

We value our own time and respect other people's. Management meetings take one hour – if you leave them open-ended they can take forever, because everyone wants to talk. In a tight time frame, you have to focus. If you're late, you'll miss some of the meeting, because it's going to start on time.

THE MOST VALUABLE POSSESSION OF ALL IS TIME

It's not just meetings – Panther Taekwondo classes always start on time too. Time is the most valuable thing on earth. When it's lost, you'll never get it back. Time is the master – you can never reclaim it. So press-ups are a punishment for students if they are late: no one likes doing press-ups!

CREATING A WINNING MENTALITY

My fighting career wasn't all winning. I can still remember my first – and worst - knock out.

My first time at the French Open Championship, I won the first round – got through quite easily, in fact. Then I was facing my second opponent, and I knew he had a very fast spinning kick in his repertoire. Whenever he competed, he knocked a few people out that way.

My coach advised me to go forward in the match – but watch out for that kick. I did that – started attacking not defending, watching carefully – and the next thing I knew, I was down. It felt as if I was at the bottom of a swimming pool.

The kick had landed so fast that I hadn't seen it coming. I was down, feeling as though I was underwater, and the referee was counting.

I'd been told that in the case of a knock-out, I should look to my corner for advice, so I looked. I saw that I was being motioned to take my time and recover before I got to my feet, so I stayed down and tried to listen to the referee's count.

*"You can judge your future
by the company you keep"*

1, 2, 3... then somehow he seemed to miss out 6 and 7 and 8... and now he was saying 9, then 10... and I had been counted out.

Everything still seemed to be underwater. Somehow I struggled to my feet and said to the referee, *"I'm ok"*. *But the referee had different ideas: he said to me firmly, "no you're not, you're out"*.

I was so dazed that I'd not heard the count properly. It was clear that I really couldn't continue, even if I'd wanted to.

I'd received a hard spinning kick to the side of my head, and when I got home I found I couldn't move my jaw. I wondered if it was broken (it wasn't). To get knocked out in a tournament like that set me back mentally – I'd never been so wiped out before and it was hard to deal with.

I discussed what had happened with my father. I even said I was thinking of stopping. But Dad just said to me: *"great is not the man who stands firm and never gets knocked down. Great is the man who is knocked down and rises again"*. He told me to stand up and get back in the next competition.

And of course, dad was right, I trained harder after that. I trained to do flash spins before attacking, to make myself harder to see. I knew that I needed to be sharper and faster than the guy I was fighting.

THE STORY OF CHARLES GORDON

"I started training with Panther Taekwondo around the age of 10 because my parents wanted me to take part in an activity to keep me fit while teaching me focus and self discipline.

"Panther Taekwondo helped to keep me focused and my trainer, Grand Master Ewan, taught me how to focus on my personal priorities in a disciplined way. This meant staying positive about the future, finding solutions to problems and, as a young male, being in the company of others who were also focussed on making something of their lives. Getting in with a bad crowd can be very harmful to young people and Grand Master Ewan's words have always stayed with me: 'You can judge your future by the company you keep'.

"Panther Taekwondo keeps my mind, body and soul refreshed"

"Above all, he taught me indomitable spirit. Even when something had gone wrong for me and I was upset and not wanting to put effort into my training, he kept me inspired.

"Of course, later on when I was working, sometimes the pressures would really build up around me. You can't get anywhere in life without being able to persist at stressful times, but you also need a place to allow you to escape that pressure and take a break. Attending Panther Taekwondo Classes was that escape.

"Training at Panther Taekwondo allows me to go through the routine of learning self-discipline, and reinforces the values of working through pain and distractions. This leaves my mind, body and soul feeling quite refreshed. Not only does it do wonders for the mind, but it also helps keep me physically fit and active, which in turns helps me keep up my energy, work hard and stay focused.

"I decided to become an estate agent, and kept myself very clear around my work goals, no matter what other people around me decided to do. I'm incredibly grateful to have been able to learn that kind of focus: it's such an important skill for success in life.

"After implementing the skills and focus that Grand Master Ewan taught me from a young age, I became a multi millionaire at the age of 25.

"The life skills I've learned have a huge impact on my estate agency business and I have used so much of Grand Master Ewan's regimented, no-nonsense business model to great effect.

"So I can confidently say that Panther Taekwondo Black Belt Academy isn't just a martial arts school. For me, it's a way of life".

LEADERSHIP AND MANAGEMENT

Our Leadership Squad Program gives students enhanced responsibility in class and teaches them to be positive role models and leaders both in class and at school.

"The experiences and responsibilities of Panther Taekwondo Leaders transfer to many other aspects of their lives"

Students explore the behaviours that exemplify good leadership and develop confidence and public speaking skills by giving oral reports on life skills related to leadership.

They learn to set an example for others in class, to help mentor junior-ranked students, and to take on a variety of leadership roles. As trusted senior leaders they also are eligible to practice advanced self-defence applications using release and restraint and pressure point control tactics.

Panther Taekwondo Junior Leadership is a program designed for students from the ages of ten who demonstrate desire, attitude and potential to become part of the Panther Taekwondo Community of Leaders. Leadership candidates are selected individually for the qualities that will make them good role models both at Taekwondo and outside.

Leadership squad members learn to have positive attitudes and behaviours in all situations. They are supported to do their best to maintain a good academic record in regular school and to be helpful at home.

As part of their training, Junior Leaders gain extra knowledge of the Panther Taekwondo curriculum and are often called on to participate in public and classroom demonstrations. They also have opportunities to increase their leadership skills by assisting other children under the supervision of a qualified instructor. As their skills improve, they are tested and move through the ranks until they can join the Panther Taekwondo Senior Leadership Team.

The experiences and responsibilities that Panther Taekwondo Leaders acquire build self-confidence and skills which are transferable to many other aspects of their lives.

Our leadership program is also built specifically for teens and young adults who wish to improve their leadership skills. While many lessons are taught with reference to Taekwondo, the skills learned in this class are versatile and encompassing enough to be used in any leadership situation at home, church, or school, and later on in adult life.

"Excuses are like arseholes — we've all got them and they all stink!"

We aim to create great people who will be able to act appropriately in any situation and who will be the future leaders of our community. Young people are taught communication skills, goal setting, classroom management and public speaking, in an effort to make them well-rounded and confident individuals who can adapt and succeed in any situation they may find themselves in.

This, on top of their regular martial arts instruction, makes them a positive force in their communities and equips them to perform effectively in many aspects of their lives.

TEAM BUILDING

The management team of Panther is all homegrown. They are people who have trained with me over minimum of 10 years and often more. This makes us a cohesive team. They have to have demonstrated commitment to Panther above personal issues.

But it doesn't have to take ten years to build a strong team. The art of Taekwondo can help you do this by offering discipline and structure.

Ninety-five percent training attendance is required – that means no small excuses are acceptable. As we say to our students: if your leg drops off on the way to training, hop along to training and you'll still be in the team.

Team members can swap phone numbers and ring each other for support, which creates positive peer pressure. So there's support from within the group as well as from leaders.

I believe in structure and authority. Children see me bow to my instructor, and so they will bow to theirs. We embed Korean traditional modes of conduct which I believe are quite simple guidelines to respect and good manners.

So when we eat together as a group on tour, we follow the traditional Korean codes. You start eating after your instructor but must finish before he or she does, so your instructor is not waiting on you to finish,

"There was no segregation of men and women in the classes – we were all treated equally and all respected"

and ensure that the glasses of senior students and instructors are never less than half full.

It's in small matters such as these that teams are bonded and real cohesion develops. We make sure that everyone is aware of those around them and can rely upon and trust their fellow team members in large and small matters. It's about interdependence: having the confidence to rely upon and trust another person.

BRENDA EMMANUS

Brenda Emmanus is currently Art, Culture and Entertainment Correspondent for BBC London News – and a double bronze medallist in Taekwondo at national level. For many years she has been an enthusiastic student of Taekwondo.

"I discovered Taekwondo while at university', she says."I had enjoyed team sports while at school but had not consciously made an effort to align myself with any specific activity while studying for my degree. I was introduced to the sport by a very dynamic instructor, Master Ebe Ghansah.

"What seduced me about Taekwondo was not only the grace and skill of participants but how democratising it was. Men and women of all ages, cultures and sizes were participating and gaining confidence while getting fit. There was no segregation of men and women in the classes – we were all treated equally and all respected. I did better than I would ever imagined over the years, gaining two bronze medals in national championships – all this in a sport I did just for a hobby!

"So when I noticed that my daughter was not enjoying sport as much as I'd anticipated she would at school, I decided to get her to try Panther Taekwondo. I was hoping that through the classes she would gain confidence as she happens to be an introvert by nature. If I'm really honest, I thought she might hate it and find it too aggressive for her nature. But my own good experiences inspired me to let her try – and to my surprise she took to it like a duck to water.

"My greatest moment so far was watching her having her medal placed over her head"

EGO IS LEFT AT THE DOOR: RESPECT IS KING

"In the last couple of years, my daughter's confidence has grown tremendously. She is now a green belt, having double graded once and achieved a silver medal in her first championships. She is extremely disciplined and focused in the class – more than I've seen her been in any other situation, and it's a joy to watch how she has integrated and socialises with her fellow 'Panthers.'

"My greatest moment so far was watching her having her medal placed over her head and her team cheering in support, and also when I caught her working out how long and what it would take for her to achieve her black belt.

"The Panther instructors are extraordinary, not only in the manner in which they share their skills but how they inspire the students to rise to become the best of themselves in all they do. Grand Master Ewan and his team are so inspirational. Grand Master Ewan in particular not only commands respect from the instructors and pupils, but also consistently has words of wisdom and inspirational gems to disperse with the students.

"Watching how children are transformed into focused, confident young athletes who believe in their ability to exceed beyond their own expectations is a joy. What is particularly special about the way Grand Master Ewan and his team operate is the family environment that manifests itself in those sessions. Ego is left at the door, respect is king! The instructors are a true testament to how authentic leaders can be found in all walks of life".

"So... what is your mission in life?"

CHAPTER FIVE:
PANTHER TAEKWONDO FOR PURPOSEFUL LIVING

Everybody needs a purpose.

So I ask everybody, *"What is your mission?"*. If they can't answer, I know we have some work to do.

What is your mission in life?

Where are you going?

How are you going to get there?

What's your end game?

What are you going to do to make your mark in this world?

Your purpose might be to start your own business, make ten million pounds before you're thirty and then become Prime Minister. Or it might be to make the community you live in stronger and more cohesive. It might be fund-raise for charity, to campaign for international justice or for animal rights. It might be make sure that your children do well in life and become the sort of people who'll take the world in the right direction in the future.

HAVE A MISSION – TO BE THE BEST YOU

So – what is your mission?

However you answer that question, there's only one real mission and it's the same one for us all. Your mission, and mine, has to be to try your

"*Competing is easy, training is hard*"

best at whatever you do, to be the best that you can possibly be. That's a great mission to have.

Your mission could be, if you're a singer, to sing a little better. When you're in the bath, sing louder. If you can walk fast, train to walk even faster. Your mission could be that you paid all your bills, created financial stability and a sound structure for your family: a house, a roof over your head, food in your belly. So many people in this world don't have that right now; to be a good provider and to create security for the next generation is a noble purpose.

Live your life to the full. Find your mission. Be the best you.

SUCCESS IS IN PREPARATION AND MINDSET

When I was a nine times British Taekwondo champion and I got to the big day... it was never that big a deal.

That's because the hard work was already done.

Preparation is power. Whatever you set out to achieve in life, it's the preparation you put in that makes the difference between success and failure.

Competing is easy – training is hard. Success is all in the preparation and mindset.

Wake up in the morning and set the tone for your day. So how are you? I'm good, I'm better than good. Start each day this way.

HOW DO WE FIND OUR PURPOSE?

To answer this question I'm going to go back to the start of this book, and the experience I had as a young boy. My dad had decided that I was going to study a martial art: that was fine. Sport was part of the culture of my family and I embraced it. Then he decided which one – it was boxing. He meant very well when he did this, and based his decision on the fact that I am his son. It must have seemed natural to him that

*"I'm a strong believer in
reflecting on the path we
choose to take in life"*

I would take after him and that for me, boxing would be also the right way to go.

At the time, I didn't disagree. I thought about it, and it seemed like a good idea. In my head, I was happy with this decision.

Then I had an experience – a much more basic, visceral event than anything that goes on between our ears. I physically experienced boxing and I rejected it. My instincts said to me: no, this is not the right thing for you to do.

I'm a strong believer in reflecting on the path we choose to take in life. But what this experience taught me is that the place to find purpose isn't in our brains at all. What my dad *thought* was right for me, and what I *thought* must be right because he was my dad and he wanted the best for me – turned out not to be right at all. When his thoughts and my thoughts came into contact with reality – everything changed.

So this is the time to ask some completely different questions. It's time for keeping it real and discovering how to live our lives in ways that are true to ourselves. Finding your purpose is the most real and powerful thing that you will ever do.

Here's some question to help you close in on your purpose in life. As you answer them – be instinctive. That means – be true to yourself.

Remember, when you manifest your purpose, it will be a gift to those around you

Try to step away from the expectations other people have of you. Try to even step away from the love and gratitude you feel towards those people. Let this decision be about you and the way you feel inside. Remember that when you have a clear sense of your purpose in life and you're living in it and making it manifest, it will become a great gift to all the people around you.

So: what would you do even if you weren't paid?

"What connects you with the most authentic you?"

What would you do for sheer love and enjoyment, and how good you feel when you are doing it? (If your answer is 'making money', that's great: what it means is that you're an entrepreneur, and that business and generating wealth is your passion! The country will always need wealth creators).

What do you love to do?

What do you feel most authentic doing?

What are you an expert in, just because you're so interested in it that somehow you always pick up information about it and then remember it?

What connects you with the most authentic you?

When you experience *'flow'*? 'Flow' is a state in which time passes by without you being aware of it because you are completely absorbed in what you are doing. What is the activity that enables you to reach it?

Somewhere in those answers lies your authenticity and your purpose in life.

So now you've found your purpose – what are you going to do about it?

FINDING ANOTHER WAY

When I walked into a tournament believing I've won, and already having seen myself win, I walked in with a huge advantage. I'd seen myself with my hands raised and the gold medal going around my neck. I'd seen it happen already. I'd imagined it. It was real to me. Then I went in there and executed it.

But things didn't always go so smoothly.

My last international fight before retirement was the French Open Championship in 1989. The end of my international career was a very

*"I stayed positive and
I found a way"*

big deal to me, and had the effect of making me more nervous before the fight than I would otherwise have been. So I trained very, very hard, and even invited my great friend and mentor, Master Kim Koren, who was based in Belgium, to come to France to train with me. I worked and worked in the week leading up to the tournament, but I was still extremely nervous.

Somehow, during that week, in all my nervous anticipation, I kicked Kim's elbow and ended up with a haematoma on my foot (that means there was a collection of blood outside the blood vessels). It was very painful and caused problems in training. But there was no stepping down from this tournament.

I wrapped up my foot carefully before the tournament began, not something which is normally permitted in Taekwondo but I cleared it with the tournament doctors and they gave me permission. The fight seemed to begin well. Then − I caught my opponent's elbow with my injured foot. The swelling began to increase and suddenly I was in agony.

But I'd got two arms and another foot.

So using the parts of my body which still remained ready to fight, I decided to approach this fight another way: instead of going for a knock-out, I would aim to win on points. I'd attack to get a point, then fight defensively to block his retaliation and try to close him down (this is called 'smothering').

So I scored a point, then smothered him, scored again, smothered again, over and over − until I won on points.

About an hour later, when the elation of my victory subsided, very bad pain did kick in again, and I realised I'd have to go to hospital. It turned out I had a cracked bone in my instep, and I finished up staying longer in France than I'd planned to receive medical treatment.

But the important thing was: I stayed positive and I found a way.

When I wake up in the morning, my wife says, "how are you?" and I say back to her, "I'm good. I'm better than good, I'm great"

Training isn't just about training your body, making your muscles stronger, developing your skills. It's about attitude.

When I wake up in the morning, my wife says, *"how are you?"* and I say back to her, *"I'm good. I'm better than good, I'm great"* – I'm not just talking to her. I'm creating a mindset in myself. If you start with the attitude, *"I'm not a morning person. I don't feel so good…"* you can only go down. Start with positivity and you'll build up higher.

A BLACK BELT IS MASTER OF THE BASICS

OK – so you know your purpose. Now – keep it simple.

Don't try to do too much at once; accept that things take time.

From the very first gradings you ever go through, you'll learn in Panther Taekwondo that before success comes effort and work. You need to learn the basics, then build from there, with vision and belief in your future success to inspire you. Master the basics first.

Taekwondo teaches a very special kind of focus. It teaches concentration and drive. It can make you unstoppable.

Here's the difference I've seen it make in the lives of three people I'm proud to know and to have helped on their journeys.

DANNY JOHN JULES

37 years a friend and student, the well-known actor and entertainer talks about getting to know Ewan, and his experiences in Panther Taekwondo.

"I first met Ewan around 37 years ago at the Pineapple Dance Centre in central London. Ewan was teaching martial arts and I was an up and coming dancer.

"Two worlds collided, dance and martial arts. Both were immensely tough on the body, needing dedication, hours of practice and a very healthy pain threshold.

"In a huge building full of dancers, two people stuck out like a sore thumb, Ewan and Steve, who had a gym in one of the studios. Naturally they were both sentenced to the basement studios to ply their trade.

"We all talked about anything that included physicality. We depended on it for our livings. We always wanted to learn. How can we get fitter, stronger, faster? Which muscles do I need to work on to jump higher? Ewan was a huge help to me in stretching my physical limits.

"Years later (having had all this private (and free!) tuition from Ewan) in 2002 I ended up doing the film Blade 2 with Wesley Snipes. You never know when someone's advice will help you in a time of need. Those were good days.

"Roll on some more years and I meet up with Ewan again through a mutual friend. That meeting ended with me making a low budget fight film called Suckerpunch. Ewan even made a cameo appearance!

"Even when Ewan was gravely sick, he never stopped. I saw it with my own eyes. And that's why I turn up when he calls me to give out certificates at his

ceremonies. I have been with him since he only had one school, and through his highs and lows. I've always admired his determination and military work ethic.

"I've seen hundreds and hundreds of kids over the years who have passed through his tutelage and mentoring. It's staggering to think that one man can have so much energy. These kids are from all walks of life and cultures. They are courteous, disciplined, hard working and above all, well mannered. I am always addressed with a 'sir'. And I'm not going to lie. It feels good.

"Our community needs to celebrate not only 'celebrity' but the real soldiers, toiling with all their hearts and souls in the trenches of urban enclaves to help give kids the head start they are going to need to negotiate the maze better known as 'The World We Live in'. You're one of the captains.

"I take my hat off to you, sir".

MASTER WAINE ROYE

"At a time when many people think that Taekwondo is simply a sport, it's good to remind ourselves of the unique spirit and discipline within it. This is what gave my life a new structure and focus.

"Growing up in a tough area rubbed off on me. I was known for my hair trigger temper. I didn't really deal with the way I felt at all: I couldn't. When I had problems, I sorted them out with my fists.

"Panther Taekwondo Black Belt Academy has helped me in many different ways. It has enabled me to grow up into someone different from that tough young man who was quick to anger, and deal more effectively with life's highs and lows. There has been more than one occasion in my life where I've had to utilise the focus and discipline acquired through my training.

"It's also helped me look after myself physically at a time when many people find this hard because of the many pressures and challenges of modern society. Looking at the physical shape of some of the people I have grown up with, I thank God that Panther Taekwondo Black Belt Academy has kept me in shape.

"At one of the saddest times in my life, back in 2007, I was very much aware of the difference my Taekwondo training was making for me. On May 19th that year, we sadly lost my dad. It was very hard on the whole family. But I found I was able to deal with my own very painful feelings and be a rock for the people around me. Looking back, I can see that this was because of the focus and mental discipline I had learnt at Panther Taekwondo.

"That's not to say I didn't feel as bad as anyone else about what I had happened, but I could also see the pain and difficulty of others and what they needed from

*"Before my martial arts training,
I could not have controlled
myself in this way"*

me at that time. When you experience deep grief, it's easy to begin to feel out of control and overwhelmed. But I found that although my own strong emotions were present, they were not overwhelming to me and I was able to deal with them. I could therefore remain aware of the whole situation around me and how other members of family were doing.

"Then, when there was an appropriate moment to take time for me, I could do that too. I know that before my martial arts training, I would not have been able to manage myself in that way.

"Through the teachings of Grand Master Ewan Briscoe and Panther Taekwondo, I and my two sons as a family have become national champions on numerous occasions and traveled around the world as martial arts competitors. After that, we became coaches and officials and referees in the sport. Finally we opened our own classes under the Panther Taekwondo Black Belt Academy brand.

"Things have progressed so well for us that my sons and I have also opened a successful after schools sports business and used that to bring Panther Taekwondo into schools.

"If Panther Taekwondo Black Belt Academy can help me turn my life around, it can surely help the future generations. So a big thanks to Grandmaster Ewan Briscoe: without this man. I am sure my own life would taken a different path".

MASTER GILBERT GRAHAM

"My love started for Taekwondo in 1986 when I was looking for another sporting hobby. One day whilst walking through Mountsfield Park, I came across a Taekwondo demonstration led by Ewan Briscoe performing a spinning kick which involved kicking an apple off a student's head. This demonstration inspired me – his flexibility, strength and technique were mind-blowing. This was the starting point for me and I was immediately attracted to the art.

"After a discussion with Ewan after the demonstration, I decided to try it and I began training at Panther Taekwondo at St Mary's Centre, Ladywell. As a new student, it felt like a long uphill journey to become a black belt but I was made to feel very welcome and the warmth of the class can be likened to a family of students from similar backgrounds.

"After the first year, I experienced a noticeable difference in my fitness levels and technical ability and started setting myself targets to move up in the grades which involved taking part in tournaments. Inspired by Ewan, I strived to take up a role in the class. I began organising social events and continued to help teaching smaller groups until I reached the grade of black belt.

"I was then given the opportunity to lead my own class, Panther Taekwondo Forest Hill. As I became more involved in Panther Taekwondo, Grand Master Ewan and I became friends and as our friendship grew, my inspiration and focus for Taekwondo grew stronger.

"I was at this point I recognised that I got more of a buzz teaching Taekwondo than I did simply doing Taekwondo. My main job up to that time has been that of a postman and driver for Royal Mail. I shared with Master Ewan my wish to get more involved in teaching, and with his encouragement I applied to do an access course in sports coaching.

"And to think – all this started from seeing a spinning kick, 30 years ago"

"I took a break from Taekwondo and went to university where I gained my degree in sports coaching. During my time at university, I joined a company called Teachsport who provide coaches to teach physical education in schools, where increasingly there are no full-time PE teachers present. This gave me the chance to combine my skills as a sports coach with that of a Taekwondo Instructor and develop good class management, which enhanced my teaching skills.

"I re-started my Taekwondo career with Master Ewan and went on to gain my master status in the art. I also established Diamond Sports Services, a subsidiary of Panther Taekwondo.

"Panther Taekwondo has taught me to never quit, confidence, self-discipline, the ability to start something new and the passion to love what you do and do what you love. I now run my own company where I give young students a chance to gain paid employment and the opportunity to enhance their skills gained through Panther Taekwondo into the working world.

"And to think – all this started from seeing a spinning kick, 30 years ago".

"When you give yourself to others, you get a lot back"

CONCLUSION: PASSING IT ON

All the best mentoring relationships work both ways. When you give yourself to others, you get a lot back.

Here are the lessons I've learned from the great people I've coached and mentored down the years.

I feel fortunate and blessed to have so much to be proud of. I take strength from my achievements. I'm lucky – and I continue to be lucky – to be able to see the difference I've made in the world. And that's a gift I'm still receiving.

I'm very much aware that I'm part of a cycle, a process. I belong with other people and together we try to make a difference and to hand on the things we've learned and to teach, mentor and support others.

Recently I watched one of my students supervising others at a grading presentation. Three years ago, this young boy couldn't walk confidently into the room, and certainly couldn't speak up for himself if you asked him a question. He'd been a fragile guy who didn't have much self-esteem, and his parents brought him along to build his self confidence and give him a more healthy sense of his self-will and control over his life.

Now he's a senior grade in the class and a high-ranking student. The next belt he achieves will be a black belt.

So as a result of this progress, he is now one of the students who will dress up in a suit and tie at the grading and help other students while they prepare for it, then at the grading he will advise and monitor what they are doing.

"*I don't need to be a great black belt, sir — I just want to be like you*"

I was really surprised at how efficient he was at this, and how vociferous he was. He used to cry when he experienced setbacks, and found training hard because he was shy and introverted. Now here he was, literally telling other students what to do and how to do it, and inputting the confidence into them that we had put into him. Now he's the epitome of what I work for and look for as I'm teaching Taekwondo.

This is the reason I would never – even if I might occasionally want to or think about retirement or just settling down a bit and working less and taking it easy – why I would *never* give up teaching Taekwondo. That moment watching him showed to me the responsibility I have in enthusing children to become better people – to become better than good and the best they can be.

I called him over - the young chap – and said to him: *'I can see that you are going to make a great black belt'*. At that point he fist-punched in the air and said: *"I don't need to be a great black belt, sir – I just want to be like you"*.

That literally brought tears to my eyes – the thought that I could come to a point in my life where I inspire someone so much that they wanted to be like me. It was immensely moving and humbling.

It brought to my mind the memory of something my dad said to me years before, when I told him that I'd created my first black belts at the academy. What he said to me was this: that now, and only now, he was really impressed.

He'd never said this to me before, because of course I hadn't been ready to hear it. But all the trophies I'd brought to him and showed him, while he'd been pleased with those and pleased for me, were things he would have expected of me. He knew, as an experienced fighter himself, that I had a winning attitude in the first place, so he wasn't surprised when I won (though of course he was happy and proud).

But what really impressed him, he said, was that now I had become an expert teaching experts – part of a tradition, with something to hand on to others.

"I'm sure if my dad had heard what that young boy said to me that day, he would have been proud, so proud"

When I heard that, I realised that I'd found my true purpose, the thing which made my life and my work valuable and lasting. It's to be part of a tradition and to hand that tradition on.

Now I've taught 300–400 black belts. I've lost count. I've taught those experts, and they in turn have taught experts: they have gone on to teach and to create black belts. It makes me feel that I'm part of a cycle, that what I've learned will be passed forward to others.

I'm sure if my dad had heard what that young boy said to me that day, he would have been proud, so proud. And the thought of making him proud still means more to me today than anything else I have achieved.

Lightning Source UK Ltd.
Milton Keynes UK
UKOW01f2237101017
310757UK00006B/404/P